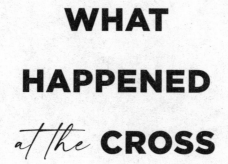

WHAT HAPPENED at the CROSS

WHAT
HAPPENED
at the CROSS

THE PRICE OF VICTORY

BILLY GRAHAM

W PUBLISHING GROUP

AN IMPRINT OF THOMAS NELSON

What Happened at the Cross

© 2021 Billy Graham Literary Foundation

Portions of this book were previously adapted and excerpted from:
How to Be Born Again (ISBN 9780849931604) © 1977, 1989
Hope for the Troubled Heart (ISBN 9780849942112) © 1991
The Reason for My Hope (ISBN 9780529105448) © 2013
Where I Am (ISBN 9780718042226) © 2015

All rights reserved. No portion of this book may be reproduced, stored in a retrieval system, or transmitted in any form or by any means—electronic, mechanical, photocopy, recording, scanning, or other—except for brief quotations in critical reviews or articles, without the prior written permission of the publisher.

Published in Nashville, Tennessee, by W Publishing, an imprint of Thomas Nelson.

Thomas Nelson titles may be purchased in bulk for educational, business, fundraising, or sales promotional use. For information, please e-mail SpecialMarkets@ThomasNelson.com.

Scripture quotations marked KJV are taken from the King James Version. Public domain.

Scripture quotations marked NASB are taken from the New American Standard Bible® (NASB). Copyright © 1960, 1962, 1963, 1968, 1971, 1972, 1973, 1975, 1977, 1995 by The Lockman Foundation. Used by permission. www.lockman.org

Scripture quotations taken from The Holy Bible, New International Version®, NIV®. Copyright © 1973, 1978, 1984, 2011 by Biblica, Inc.® Used by permission of Zondervan. All rights reserved worldwide. www.Zondervan.com. The "NIV" and "New International Version" are trademarks registered in the United States Patent and Trademark Office by Biblica, Inc.®

Scripture quotations marked NLT are taken from the Holy Bible, New Living Translation. © 1996, 2004, 2015 by Tyndale House Foundation. Used by permission of Tyndale House Publishers, Inc., Carol Stream, Illinois 60188. All rights reserved.

Scripture quotations marked NKJV are taken from the New King James Version®. Copyright © 1982 by Thomas Nelson. Used by permission. All rights reserved.

Scripture quotations marked PHILLIPS are from The New Testament in Modern English by J. B. Phillips. Copyright © 1960, 1972 J. B. Phillips. Administered by the Archbishops' Council of the Church of England. Used by permission.

Any internet addresses, phone numbers, or company or product information printed in this book are offered as a resource and are not intended in any way to be or to imply an endorsement by Thomas Nelson, nor does Thomas Nelson vouch for the existence, content, or services of these sites, phone numbers, companies, or products beyond the life of this book.

ISBN 978-0-7852-6647-1 (audiobook)
ISBN 978-0-7852-6633-4 (eBook)
ISBN 978-0-7852-6568-9 (TP)

Library of Congress Cataloging-in-Publication Data

ISBN 978-0-7852-6568-9

Printed in the United States of America

21 22 23 24 25 TRM 10 9 8 7 6 5 4 3 2 1

CONTENTS

FOREWORD

I f ever you should doubt the love of God, take a long, deep look at the cross of the Lord Jesus, for in the cross you find the expression of God's love."

My father wrote this in his classic book *Peace with God* in 1953, and the gospel message he preached over the next seven decades never changed.

From the time he stepped into the pulpit as a young Bible student as a guest preacher at a small church to the last message he preached on his ninety-fifth birthday which aired on Fox News around the world, his message was *The Cross of Jesus Christ*. Why? Because God's message never changes.

What happened at the cross is what makes it possible for people to turn from sin and find God's salvation through the perfect sacrifice His only Son made for *all*, just outside the gates of Jerusalem.

My own decision to make Jesus Savior and Lord of my life also happened overlooking this ancient city, where I knelt and prayed asking God to forgive me of my sin. That very night Christ saved my soul and transformed my life.

I had been with my father in Switzerland only two weeks before my trip to Israel. He knew the spiritual battle that was raging within me though I did not completely understand.

As we walked along Lake Geneva on my twenty-second birthday, he put his hand on my shoulder and said, "Franklin, your mother and I sense there is a struggle going on in your life."

The truth of his words startled me. I thought I had done a good job in covering up my sin. He said, "You're going to have to make a choice either to accept Christ or reject Him."

His challenge led me straight to the foot of the cross, where sinners can find forgiveness and peace and a purpose to live for Him. But it wasn't until I arrived in Jerusalem a few days later that the Holy Spirit brought me to my knees in repentance. And my life has never been the same.

Many years have passed, but still I find myself reliving the memory of my own journey to the foot of the cross. I thank the Lord for changing my life and helping me treasure the heritage of watching my parents live out testimonies for the Lord at home and before the watchful eyes of the world.

They provided the security of home in the mountains of North Carolina, but they also desired that I would see the world through God's eyes. Still today, there are remembrances that have a profound impact on me.

———

A few days before my mother went to Heaven, I was standing at her bedside, missing the twinkle in her eyes that had always brought joy. I wondered if she was recalling some of these same memories.

My mother's bedroom was a wonderful place of reflection, sort of a walk-in curio filled with pictures, books, and an array of knickknacks. But the most memorable artifact hung above her Bible study desk—a crown of thorns—given to her by the mayor of the city of Jerusalem.

In the declining days when Mama's pain intensified, she often asked to be turned toward the desk so that she could gaze at the crown of thorns. Living a life of physical pain reminded her of the most excruciating pain endured by her Savior on the cross. It was so like her to turn attention always to the things of God, and the impact of her example is branded in memory.

———

I learned from watching and listening to my father also. He had a way of connecting with hearts beyond the stark lights and probing cameras. No matter how intense the spotlight, he zeroed in on God's message. Like a laser beam, he pointed others to the cross.

When it came time for the invitation, my father called on people to respond, but it wasn't only to those in the great stadiums of the world. As thousands streamed down to gather in front of the platform, my father would turn his piercing eyes to a camera and say, "For those watching by television, if you feel a tug at your heart, if you hear a small voice calling to you, don't ignore it. That is the voice of God calling your name to come to Him."

My father peered into the faces of aching souls, bidding them to the foot of the cross. This, he said, is the greatest battleground—making the decision to accept or reject Jesus as Savior. His voice would reverberate through the speakers:

"For God so loved the world that He gave His only begotten Son, that whoever believes in Him should not perish but have everlasting life" (John 3:16 NKJV).

What are the results to such an invitation? Souls won for Christ and bound for eternal life in Heaven.

This is the message of the cross—Jesus died to save sinners.

This is why Jesus went to the cross—for you and for me. When you gaze at the cross, remember what happened there.

———

When HarperCollins Christian Publishers asked about compiling a book of some of my father's messages on the cross, I thought, *Wow! That would take several volumes, because my father never preached a sermon in which he didn't focus on what happened more than two thousand years ago at the cross on a place called Mount Calvary.*

In this special collection, you will see the light of God's glory shine upon the cross of His Son, the One whom mankind crucified. Imagine the blood streaming down Jesus' face from the thorns that pierced His brow as He hung there; His precious blood poured out for the sins of the world.

You may ask what is so hopeful about this gruesome scene; the answer is simple yet profound: God "cancelled the record of the charges against us and took it away by nailing it to the cross" (Col. 2:14 NLT).

Jesus conquered sin and death and left the tomb empty by His resurrection. The cross is the symbol of the immeasurable love of God, and He offers this victorious gift to the world.

There are people all around us today who need Jesus. Ask the Lord to help you identify someone whom you may lead to the foot of the cross. Don't put it off.

The Bible says, "Exhort one another daily, while it is called 'Today'" (Heb. 3:13 NKJV), and "Behold, now is the accepted time; behold, now is the day of salvation" (2 Cor. 6:2–3 NKJV).

May God bless you as you consider *What Happened at the Cross* because Jesus is the One who paid *The Price of Victory!*

Franklin Graham

CHAPTER 1

WHERE IS JESUS?

On the cross Jesus took upon Himself
every sin we've ever committed . . . and
during our lifetime here on earth we must
decide where we stand with Him.

Lifetime Television Network showcased the forty-foot glass cross as a camera crew entered The Billy Graham Library to tape a program highlighting it as a point of interest in the city of Charlotte, North Carolina. My colleague met the show's cohost, Kristy Villa, and explained what visitors might experience while there, drawing attention to the many crosses displayed throughout the tour known as *The Journey of Faith*.

Halfway through the presentation, Villa said with a sense of awe, "I see all the crosses, but where is Jesus?" The colleague smiled and said, "He's in Heaven, and He is also present in the lives of those who believe in Him and follow Him as their personal Lord and Savior."

The journalist threw her hands around her face and exclaimed, "Oh, that's right! Some worship a crucifix, but Christians worship a risen Christ." After a moment, Villa said, "I have been in church my whole life, but I have never heard the emphasis put on an empty cross."

She may not have realized it, but she had just proclaimed the heart of the Gospel and later told her viewers,

"This destination is a place you must come and see!"[1] When I heard this marvelous report, it made my heart leap, and I thought about the words of the psalmist: "Come and see what God has done . . . for mankind!" (Psa. 66:5 NIV).

The question we must all answer is, "What does Jesus' work on the cross and His resurrection mean, and what does it mean to be saved?"

The resurrection story of Jesus Christ is what gives meaning and power to the cross. What a failure Christianity would be if it could not carry our hopes beyond the coldness and depths of the grave. You see, the resurrection means the salvation of our souls.

What does the resurrection mean to you, and has it changed your life? Many have never thought about it. Some believe that Jesus died leaving a legacy of "Do good to your neighbor," never believing that He was raised from the dead. Others think the resurrection was a hoax. There are those who question whether Jesus even existed.

True believers in Jesus Christ have no doubt that He lived among us, died for our sins on the cross, and after three days was resurrected to life, conquering the sting of death, and offering the human race the greatest gift—His sacrificial and saving love.

Many people do not fully grasp the impact that the crucified and risen Christ makes upon the human heart. How do I know this? Because there is no change in them.

Ask yourself: "What do I believe about the empty cross and the empty tomb?" The foot of the empty cross is the place of salvation from sin, and the empty tomb illuminates with the light that brings the redeemed soul to its ultimate destination—eternal life. Acceptance of Jesus' sacrifice, or rejection of it, determines the future life of every person. If you do not believe that Jesus died for you, then you will remain the same, being gripped by sin and dying by its penalty, with certainty of eternal judgment in Hell and banishment from God. But if you believe that Jesus rose from the grave, achieving victory over the cross of death, and you accept that He paid your penalty, you will never be the same.

THE EMPTY CROSS IS FULL OF HOPE

The cross represents doom for sin and hope for sinners. It condemns sin and cleanses souls. The cross is where Jesus was crucified in our place and where Christ brings resurrection life to mankind. The bloodstained cross is gruesome to some, but the empty cross is full of hope.

Satan, overly eager to thwart God's purposes, overstepped his bounds, and God turned what seemed to be life's greatest tragedy into history's greatest triumph. The death of Christ, perpetrated by evil men, was thought by them to be the end, but His grave became a doorway to victory.

The resurrection empowers faith in Jesus Christ. If I did not believe that Christ overcame death on the cross and bodily rose from the grave, I would have quit preaching years ago. I am absolutely convinced that Jesus is living at this moment at the right hand of God the Father and He reigns in my heart. I believe it by faith, and I believe it by evidence found in the Scriptures.

Luke, a physician and disciple of Jesus, was one of the most brilliant men of his day. He made this startling statement about the resurrection in the book of Acts: "He . . . presented Himself alive after His suffering by many infallible proofs, being seen by them during forty days and speaking of the things pertaining to the kingdom of God" (Acts 1:3).

These "infallible proofs" have been debated for two thousand years. Many people have come to know the truth while they tried to prove Jesus' resurrection a lie and failed. Others ignore the facts recorded in the best-selling book of all time, the Bible.

DEFINING HISTORY

Larry King, television and radio host, a friend of mine for many years, was once asked what historical figure he would most want to interview. His answer? Jesus. "I would like to ask Him if He was indeed virgin-born. The answer to that question would define history for me."[2]

My response is always that Jesus *was* virgin-born because the Bible says so. The angel appeared to Joseph and said, "Do not be afraid to take Mary home as your wife, because what is conceived in her is from the Holy Spirit. She will give birth to a son, and you are to give him the name Jesus, because he will save his people from their sins" (Matt. 1:20–21 NIV).

The virgin birth is a stumbling block for many because they refuse to believe God's Word as evidence. You cannot believe in someone if you do not believe their words.

Jesus was born of a virgin, fulfilling prophecy.

Jesus was crucified on a cross, fulfilling prophecy.

Jesus died for the sins of mankind, fulfilling prophecy.

Jesus was buried in a borrowed tomb, fulfilling prophecy.

Jesus was raised from the dead, fulfilling prophecy.

Jesus ascended into the Heavens, also fulfilling prophecy.

And this same Jesus will come again one day in fulfillment of prophecy.

This is the hope and certainty of all those who believe in Him.

You may say, "Well, I don't believe." I would ask you this simple question: "Why?" Many people do not believe that Jesus ever existed, much less died and rose again, yet the calendar uses the birth of Jesus as the central point of time.

Why? Because He came to earth, He died and rose again, and He is coming back. Jesus has defined history, giving hope for our tomorrows.

While much of the world challenges those of the Christian faith to prove the actual existence of Jesus, a post on a prominent atheist website states that denying Jesus existed is like "saying . . . somebody willfully ignores the overwhelming evidence." Another says that "if he didn't exist, we'll never be able to prove it."[3]

WHY QUESTION THE FACTS?

The Old Testament predicted Christ's birth, death, and resurrection, and the New Testament documents the fulfillment of these prophecies, yet many people reject this truth. Yet, the biographies of so many others are believed when they were written long after their deaths.

Alexander the Great's biography, for instance, was written four hundred years after he died, so its author obviously never knew him. But Alexander's legacy lives on while people doubt the life of Christ as documented by the Gospel writers who walked with Jesus.[4]

Many people through the centuries never had a record of their own births. Yet the existence of Jesus is still called into question despite the intricate genealogy recorded in the Bible that has stood the test of time. Skeptics question His existence because of the "silent" years from age twelve to thirty. Yet the Bible documents great numbers of eyewitness accounts of His birth, His Person, His ministry, His death, and His bodily resurrection.

Did you know some today question whether William Shakespeare wrote the plays that bear his name? Why?

Because "not one of Shakespeare's original manuscripts survived."[5]

Many scholars claim that a "practical, down-to-earth rustic from the English outback . . . lacked the sophistication . . . and depth of knowledge to produce a great body of brilliant work."[6] A well-known Shakespearean actor stated in a *Washington Times* article, "I'm pretty convinced our playwright wasn't that fellow."[7]

Some see Shakespeare as a legend, a pseudonym, because there are no documents dating his birth or what Shakespeare did between the 1580s and 1592;[8] there are simply no accounts of his life during this time. His biography is peppered with suppositions and possibilities, yet "Shakespeare is the second most quoted writer in the English language—after the various writers of the Bible."[9]

Does that surprise you? It did me. Shakespeare's work is acclaimed in the literary world as genius, proving the truth of the famous eulogy by his fellow poet Ben Jonson: "He was not of an age, *but for all time!*"[10]

A very credible online article entitled "How We Know That Shakespeare Wrote Shakespeare" invites the reader to consider a number of historical facts, one being that the playwright's "contemporaries knew who he was, and there was never any doubt in the minds of those who knew him."[11] The authors conclude:

How do we know that Shakespeare wrote Shakespeare? We know because the historical record tells us so, strongly and unequivocally. The historical evidence demonstrates that one and the same man, William Shakespeare of Stratford-upon-Avon, was . . . William Shakespeare the author of the plays and poems that bear his name. . . .

[Those who assert otherwise] must rely solely upon speculation about what they think the "real" author *should* have been like, because they cannot produce one historical fact to bolster their refusal to accept who that author actually *was*. No matter how they try to ignore it or explain it away, the historical record—all of it—establishes William Shakespeare of Stratford-upon-Avon as the author of the works traditionally attributed to him.[12]

In his last will and testament, revised one month before his death, Shakespeare stated:

In the name of God . . . I William Shakespeare of Stratford upon Avon . . . in perfect health and memory, God be praised, do make and ordain this my last will and testament in manner and form following—that is to say, first, I commend my soul into the hands of God my Creator, hoping and assuredly believing, through the merits of Jesus Christ my Saviour, to be made partaker of life everlasting.[13]

Engraved on his tombstone are these words:

Good friend, for Jesus' sake forbear. . . .

Blest be the man that spares these stones,

And curst be he that moves my bones.[14]

"Though it was customary to dig up the bones from previous graves to make room for others, Shakespeare's remains are still undisturbed."[15]

I never met the great playwright, of course, but I believe he existed. His work has remained for this age, but his *remains*, by his own admission, are in the grave, awaiting the next great and monumental event of all time, the return of Jesus Christ. Jesus, not Shakespeare, is the One who is "not of an age, but for all time." Jesus Himself said: "Behold, I am coming quickly . . . I am . . . the Beginning and the End, the First and the Last" (Rev. 22:12–13).

You will never meet Shakespeare in this life because he is dead. But you can meet Jesus Christ in this life because He lives! The marks of His sacrifice on the cross are found in human hearts. Most gravestones bear the words: "Here lie the remains of . . ." But from Christ's tomb came the living words of an angel, declaring: "He is not here, but is risen!"

Jesus' tomb is history's only empty grave. Christianity has no dusty remains of the Savior to venerate, not a tomb or shrine of His to worship.

Many lawyers and jurists of history became convinced that the resurrection of Jesus Christ is a great and attested fact of history. John Singleton Copley, Lord Lyndhurst, considered one of the greatest legal minds in nineteenth-century Britain, stated it this way: "I know pretty well what evidence is; and I tell you, such evidence as that for the Resurrection [of Christ] has never broken down yet."[16]

Simon Greenleaf of Harvard University was one of "the finest writers and best esteemed legal authorities in [the nineteenth] century,"[17] and his 1842 text *A Treatise on the Law of Evidence* is still considered a classic.[18] In his book *Testimony of the Evangelists*, he approached the matter of Christ's resurrection from the standpoint of fact and evidence and concluded, "It was therefore impossible that [the Gospel writers] could have persisted in affirming the truths they have narrated, had not Jesus actually rose from the dead."[19]

Dr. William Lyon Phelps, beloved professor of English literature at Yale University for many years, declared, "The historical evidence for the resurrection [of Christ] is stronger than any other miracle."[20]

These statements are from leading intellectuals who have studied the matter from the standpoint of valid evidence, so the voice of the scholar harmonizes with that of the angels and the disciples to declare in certainty today: "Christ the Lord is risen today."[21]

There is more evidence that Jesus rose from the dead than there is that Julius Caesar ever lived or that Alexander the Great died at the age of thirty-three. It is strange that historians will accept thousands of facts for which they can produce only shreds of evidence. But in the face of the overwhelming evidence of the resurrection of Jesus Christ, they cast a skeptical eye and hold intellectual doubts. The trouble with these people is that they do not *want* to believe. Their spiritual vision is so blinded, and they are so completely prejudiced, that they cannot accept the glorious fact of the resurrection of Christ on Bible testimony alone.

While many institutions are reluctant to authenticate biblical accounts, the Smithsonian Institution states:

The Bible, in particular the historical books of the Old Testament, are as accurate historical documents as any that we have from antiquity and are in fact more accurate than many of the Egyptian, Mesopotamian, or Greek histories. These Biblical records can be and are used in archeological work. For the most part, historical events described took place and the peoples cited really existed.[22]

The world of science cannot unequivocally deny the Bible, and neither can history, based on the evidence of eyewitness accounts. Here is what the Bible says:

For I delivered to you first of all which I also received . . . that Christ died for our sins according to the Scriptures, and that He was buried, and that He rose again the third day according to the Scriptures, and that He was seen by Cephas [Peter], then by the twelve. After that He was seen by over five hundred brethren at once, of whom the greater part remain to the present, but some have fallen asleep. (1 Cor. 15:3–6)

And what about the fact that when Jesus breathed His last, there was a great earthquake and graves opened, and many dead people were raised to life? If you had been there and witnessed your loved ones walking around after you had buried them, would you believe? Would it change your life?

Satan is on the move to discredit God's Word and the resurrection. He plays with our minds, causing us to doubt, just as he did with Eve in the garden so long ago. His tactics have not changed. Jesus said, "My words will by no means pass away" (Luke 21:33).

There is no middle ground when it comes to Jesus Christ. You either believe Him and live for Him or reject Him and live for yourself. Satan relentlessly whispers in your ear, trying to plant doubt in your mind about the truth.

For those who have not answered the question, "Where is Jesus?" Satan wants you to reject the fact that Jesus lives today in the hearts of those who believe in Him. For those who have settled the question, Satan wants you to doubt Christ's power in your life. It is important to know who the enemy is and how his battle plan unfolds. From the beginning Satan longed to rob God of His rightful place, His throne of glory and power. Satan will never accomplish his goal in the big picture, but he can accomplish it in our lives if we let him.

DOWN THROUGH THE CENTURIES

Jesus once asked His disciples a challenging question:

"Who do men say that I am?" So they answered, "John the Baptist; but some say, Elijah; and others, one of the prophets." He said to them, "But who do you say that I am?" Peter answered and said to Him, "You are the Christ." (Mark 8:27–29)

As you read these pages, do you sense Jesus asking, "Who do you say that I am?"

Well, it is interesting to go back through the centuries and consider what others have said about Jesus. Skeptics claim that the Scriptures are not believable, yet testimonies about Jesus' life and resurrection come from historians, philosophers, scientists, churchmen, and, yes, even atheists. Evidence is substantiated in scrolls of antiquity, quill-stained parchments, and modern communications.

Centuries of history document testimony concerning Jesus. As early as the first century, a Jewish historian named Flavius Josephus, whose personal acceptance of Jesus as Messiah is debatable, confirmed the impact Jesus Christ made in the hearts of His followers:

About this time there lived Jesus, a wise man. . . . He won over many Jews and many of the Greeks. He was the Messiah. When Pilate . . . had condemned him to be crucified, those who had in the first place come to love him did not give up their affection for him. On the third day he appeared to them restored to life, for the prophets of God had prophesied these and countless other marvelous things about him. And the tribe of the Christians, so called after him, has still to this day not disappeared.[23]

Justin Martyr and Tertullian, second-century historians and philosophers, refer to the existence of an official document in Rome from Pontius Pilate that speaks of Jesus' crucifixion: "Tiberius . . . having himself received intelligence from Palestine of events which had clearly shown the truth of Christ's divinity, brought the matter before the senate, with his own decision in favor of Christ."[24]

In fact, the acts of Pontius Pilate related to Jesus' trial, crucifixion, and resurrection are documented by quite a few early sources, most notably Justin, Tertullian, and Eusebius, who reported on their examination of letters from Pilate to Tiberius Caesar regarding the trial and execution of Jesus.[25] While many call into question the authenticity of such resources, it is not inconceivable to believe that the most dramatic event in Israel would not be properly documented by the ruling procurator of Judea, who would be expected to give full account to the emperor of Rome.

Even negative historical documents carry evidence of the truth and power of the biblical story. The fourth-century Roman emperor named Julian the Apostate opposed Christians and wrote of them disparagingly, but even his insults bear witness:

Jesus . . . has now been celebrated about three hundred

years having done nothing in his lifetime worthy of fame, unless anyone thinks it is a very great work to heal lame and blind people and exorcise demoniacs. . . . These impious Galileans not only feed their own poor, but ours also; welcoming them into their agape [love].[26]

The end of Julian's life bears an interesting "backward" testimony as well. He was fatally wounded during a battle with the Persians and died sometime later. Many accounts claim that as he held up his dagger toward the sky, his last words were, "Vicisti, Galilaee," which translates, "Thou hast conquered, O Galilean."[27]

The Athenian philosopher Socrates lived four centuries before Jesus and was engaged in the pursuit of truth. His most famous quote is "I know that I know nothing."[28] Though this famous Greek left no written word behind him, we know about him because his followers, particularly Plato, "wrote their recollections of what he had said and done."[29] One writer has noted that "Socrates taught for 40 years, Plato for 50, Aristotle for 40, and Jesus for only 3. Yet the influence of Christ's 3-year ministry infinitely transcends the impact left by the combined 130 years of teaching from these men who were among the greatest philosophers of all antiquity."[30]

This opinion echoes that of Augustine in the fourth century: "I have read in Plato and Cicero sayings that are very wise and very beautiful; but I never read in either of them: 'Come unto me all ye that labor and are heavy laden.'"[31]

Many centuries later, in the 1700s, the influential Swiss French philosopher Jean Jacques Rousseau wrote admiringly of Jesus:

If the life and death of Socrates are those of a sage, the life and death of Jesus are those of a God. Shall we suppose the evangelic history a mere fiction? . . . it bears not the marks of fiction. On the contrary, the history of Socrates, which nobody presumes to doubt, is not so well attested as that of Jesus Christ.[32]

And since the truth of Christ is absolute, His life and death confirm the fulfillment of His resurrection.

Johann Sebastian Bach's masterpieces of the eighteenth century were centered on Christ's death and resurrection. When Bach died in 1750, it was said that he "yield[ed] up his blessed soul to his saviour."[33]

The emperor Napoleon in the early nineteenth century spoke convincingly of the truth of the Bible's claims about Jesus:

I know men, and I tell you that Jesus Christ is not a

[mere] man. Superficial minds see a resemblance between Christ and the founders of empires and the gods of other religions. That resemblance does not exist. . . . I search in vain in history to find the similar to Jesus Christ, or anything which can approach the gospel. Neither history, nor humanity, nor the ages, nor nature offer me anything with which I am able to compare it or to explain it. Here everything is extraordinary. The more I consider the gospel, the more I am assured that there is nothing there which is not beyond the march of events and above the human mind. . . . You speak of Caesar, of Alexander; of their conquests, and of the enthusiasm which they enkindled in the hearts of their soldiers. But can you conceive of a dead man making conquests, with an army faithful and entirely devoted to his memory. My armies have forgotten me, even while living, as the Carthaginian army forgot Hannibal. Such is our power! . . . Alexander, Caesar, Charlemagne, and myself founded empires. But upon what did we rest the creations of our genius? Upon *force*. Jesus Christ alone founded his empire upon *love*; and at this hour millions of men would die for him.[34]

Vincent van Gogh, the great Dutch painter and mysterious personality, commented "Christ . . . is more of an artist than the artists; he works in the living spirit and the living flesh, he makes *men* instead of statues."[35]

Lord Byron, the British Romantic poet from a generation earlier, stated even more concisely, "If ever man was God or God man, Jesus Christ was both."[36]

And classic science-fiction novelist H. G. Wells wrote in 1935:

It is interesting and significant that a historian, without any theological bias whatever, should find that he cannot portray the progress of humanity honestly without giving a foremost place to a penniless teacher from Nazareth. . . . [One] like myself, who does not even call himself a Christian, finds the picture centering irresistibly around the life and character of this most significant man. . . . the world began to be a different world from the day that [His] doctrine was preached.[37]

Why is this? Because Jesus is the Word of God in flesh. He was resurrected to fulfill that living Word, and He lives today.

The prolific and eloquent nineteenth-century novelist Charles Dickens wrote, "I now most solemnly impress upon you the truth and beauty of the Christian religion, as it came from Christ Himself."[38]

The American statesman Daniel Webster said, "If I could comprehend [Jesus Christ], he could be no greater than myself. Such is my sense of sin, and consciousness of my inability to save myself, that I feel I need a superhuman Saviour."[39] A short time before he died in 1852, he wrote, "My heart has always assured and reassured me, that the Gospel of Jesus Christ must be a Divine Reality. . . . The whole history of man proves it."[40]

There is no Gospel without the certainty of the resurrection. That's what makes the Gospel the Gospel and its certain hope.

American historian George Bancroft, U.S. secretary of the navy and founder of the U.S. Naval Academy at Annapolis in the 1800s, said, "I find the name of Jesus Christ written on the top of every page of modern history."[41]

David Strauss, a German theologian and a most bitter opponent of the supernatural elements of the Gospels, whose work may have done more to destroy faith in Christ than the writings of any other man in modern times, confessed toward the end of his life that "This Christ . . . is *historical*, not mythical; is an individual, no mere symbol. . . . He remains the highest model of religion within the reach of our thought; and no perfect piety is possible without his presence in the heart."[42]

Swiss-born theologian and historian Philip Schaff, who wrote in response to Strauss, added this assessment:

This Jesus of Nazareth, without money and arms, conquered more millions than Alexander, Caesar, Mohammed, and Napoleon; without science and learning, he shed more light on things human and divine than all philosophers and scholars combined; without the eloquence of schools, he spoke such words of life as were never spoken before or since, and produced effects which lie beyond the reach of any orator or poet; without writing a single line, he set more pens in motion, and furnished themes for more sermons, orations, discussions, learned volumes, works of art, and sweet songs of praise, than the whole army of great men of ancient and modern times.[43]

This man, Jesus, lived among us, died at our sinful hands, and rose from the grave to give us life everlasting.

Ernest Renan, French historian from the nineteenth century and an expert in ancient civilizations, said, "all history is incomprehensible without [Christ]. . . . whatever may be the unexpected phenomena of the future, Jesus will not be surpassed. . . . all the ages will proclaim that, among the sons of men, there is none born who is greater than Jesus."[44]

Sholem Asch, a Polish-born Yiddish writer from the early twentieth century, wrote,

Jesus Christ is to me the outstanding personality of all time, all history, both as Son of God and as Son of Man. Everything he ever said or did has value for us today and that is something you can say of no other man, dead or alive. There is no easy middle ground to stroll upon. You either accept Jesus or reject him. You can analyze Mohammed and . . . Buddha, but don't try it with him.[45]

Asch also penned this memorable line about Jesus: "He became the Light of the World. Why shouldn't I, a Jew, be proud of that?"[46]

When the Pharisees told Jesus to silence His followers for proclaiming Him the King of Glory, Jesus said, "I tell you that if these should keep silent, the stones would immediately cry out" (Luke 19:40). Archaeology is a sought after adventure. Some enter this field, studying antiquities, to disprove the Bible. But when many brush the dust of the earth from their knees, they confess that Jesus is Lord! The very rocks do cry out that Jesus lives.

Archaeologist William Albright, born in Chile of missionary parents, stated, "There can be no doubt that archaeology has confirmed the substantial historicity of Old Testament tradition."[47]

Jewish archaeologist Nelson Glueck said, "It may be stated categorically that no archaeological discovery has ever controverted a Biblical reference. Scores of archaeological findings have been made which confirm in clear outline or in exact detail historical statements in the Bible."[48]

Where do you stand among these men of history when it comes to Jesus Christ?

THE JESUS EFFECT

As communication tools became more widely available, documenting history became easier, and the twentieth century gave us libraries of information that will keep generations busy until Jesus Himself returns, confirming the overwhelming evidence found in the Bible, of which the apostle John wrote: "And there are also many other things that Jesus did, which if they were written one by one, I suppose that even the world itself could not contain" (John 21:25).

Kenneth Scott Latourette, former president of the American Historical Society, stated:

Even if we did not have the four brief accounts which we call the Gospels we could gain a fairly adequate impression of him and of the salient points of his life, teachings, death, and resurrection from references in letters of his followers written within a generation of his death. . . .

It is evidence of his importance, of the effect that [Jesus] has had upon history and, presumably, of the baffling mystery of his being that no other life ever lived on this planet has evoked so huge a volume of literature among so many peoples and languages, and that, far from ebbing, the flood continues to mount . . . Some characteristics stand out so distinctly in the accounts . . . that they are a guarantee of authenticity, so obviously are they from life and not invented or even seriously distorted . . . [49]

Mahatma Gandhi of India said that Jesus, "a man who was completely innocent, offered himself as a sacrifice for the good of others, including his enemies, and became the ransom of the world. It was a perfect act."[50]

Orthodox Jewish scholar Pinchas Lapide said, "I accept the resurrection of Easter Sunday not as an invention of the community of disciples, but as a historical event."[51]

Dr. Charles Malik, past president of the United Nations General Assembly and someone I was privileged to know, wrote "These Things I Believe," which included this memorable line about Jesus: "His words are wonderful; his acts, including his resurrection, were wonderful; but he himself is far more wonderful. . . . he said what he said, and did what he did, only because he was who he said he was!"[52] Dr. Malik is also quoted asking, "Having fully realized that the whole world is dissolving before our very eyes, it is impossible to ask a more far-reaching question than this: 'Do you believe in Jesus Christ?'"[53]

Even *Newsweek* magazine editor Kenneth Woodward, with whom I have had the privilege of speaking to many times, wrote at the turn of the twenty-first century and the birth of a new millennium:

Historians did not record [Jesus'] birth. Nor, for thirty years, did anyone pay him much heed. A Jew from the Galilean hill country with a reputation for teaching and healing, he showed up at the age of thirty-three in Jerusalem during Passover. In three days, he was arrested, tried and convicted of treason, then executed like the commonest of criminals. His followers said that God raised him from the dead. Except among those who believed in him, the event passed without notice.

Two thousand years later, the centuries themselves are

measured from the birth of Jesus of Nazareth. At the end of [1999], calendars in India and China, like those in Europe, America and the Middle East, will register the dawn of the third millennium. . . . the birth of Jesus . . . number[s] the days for Christians and non-Christians alike. For Christians, Jesus is the hinge on which the door of history swings, the point at which eternity intersects with time, the Savior who redeems time by drawing all things to himself. As the second millennium draws to a close, nearly a third of the world's population claims to be his followers.[54]

Some years ago, I was invited to have coffee with Konrad Adenauer before he retired as the chancellor of Germany. He asked me, "What is the most important thing in the world?" Before I could answer, he gave the right answer and said, "The resurrection of Jesus Christ. If Jesus Christ is alive, then there is hope for the world. If Jesus Christ is in the grave, then I don't see the slightest glimmer of hope on the horizon."

Legendary actor Charlton Heston recorded the famous statement, "There's been more ink—and blood—spilled over this man since they nailed Him to the cross than over any single human being in history."[55]

Even today in the twenty-first century, throngs of

people acclaim the newly rediscovered Leonardo da Vinci fifteenth-century painting entitled *Savior of the World*. The piece had been lost for five hundred years, disguised by layers of overpainting, and was painstakingly restored before going on exhibit in London in 2001. When asked, "How can we know this is a da Vinci?" the answer was because art experts say so.[56]

Do great choirs and symphonies question the brilliant composer when singing or playing George Frideric Handel's *Messiah*? For more than 270 years, audiences have listened to this magnificent composition. The text for the music was compiled from the Bible by Handel's friend Charles Jennens, who chose 1 Timothy 3:16 for *Messiah*'s epigraph: "God was manifested in the flesh, justified in the Spirit, seen by angels, preached among the Gentiles, believed on in the world, received up to glory."[57]

When the oratorio was first performed in 1742, a member of the audience expressed gratitude to Handel for "producing such a wonderful piece of 'entertainment.' 'Entertainment!' Handel replied. 'My purpose was not to entertain, but to teach them something.'"[58] And for centuries now Handel's message has resonated in hearts, proclaiming that Jesus is the Lord who died and rose again. A soaring soprano solo in the *Messiah* masterpiece combines Job 19 and 1 Corinthians 15 to proclaim:

I know that my Redeemer liveth . . .

For now is Christ risen from the dead.[59]

Elvis Presley, who died in 1977, still ranks as one of America's most successful performers, filling arenas around the world via multimedia presentations. I remember seeing a clip from a concert where someone handed him a crown. Elvis stopped his song and said, "I'm not the King. There's only one King, and that's Jesus Christ." I also remember hearing international British pop icon Cliff Richard, who did a film for us some years ago, say that "no man can follow Christ and go astray."

THE LEAP OF FAITH TO ETERNAL LIFE

In October 1929, the *Saturday Evening Post* published a land-mark interview with the great physicist and mathematician Albert Einstein. I find his response to questions of Jesus as a historical figure simply breathtaking. He answered, "I am a Jew, but I am enthralled by the luminous figure of the Nazarene. . . . No one can read the Gospels without feeling the actual presence of Jesus. His personality pulsates in every word. No myth is filled with such life."[60]

While no one knows if Einstein ever made Jesus the Lord of his life, he did say this near the end of his life:

If you ask me to prove what I believe, I can't. . . . The mind can proceed only so far upon what it knows and can prove. There comes a point where the mind takes a leap . . . and comes out upon a higher plane of knowledge, but can never prove how it got there. All great discoveries have involved such a leap.[61]

This, my friend, may be the point in time for your higher plane—relying on more than others' testimonies and completely on faith in God alone because of what He says about Himself. "Most assuredly, I say to you, before Abraham was, I AM" (John 8:58). This leap of faith is given when you speak the name of Jesus in sincere truth, realizing that you are Hell-bound without His forgiving grace and mercy. Ask Him to look into your barren heart and your hungry soul and fill it with the faith to believe that He will change you. No matter how much knowledge you gather, no matter how much proof you accumulate, you will never know the Lord Jesus Christ without taking the certain leap of faith that salvation comes only from Him. "Now faith is confidence in what we hope for and assurance about what we do not see. This is what the ancients were commended for" (Heb. 11:1–2 NIV).

The question remains: What have you decided about Jesus Christ? There is no such thing as staying neutral. Peter Larson wrote, "Despite our efforts to keep Him out, God intrudes. The life of Jesus is bracketed by two impossibilities: a virgin's womb and an empty tomb.'"[62]

There are many among us today who acknowledge Jesus as a historical figure. Many even claim to follow Him, but their lives do not reflect a change in their thinking or in their behavior or whether the Holy Spirit reigns within them, enabling them to think godly thoughts and behave in a way that honors the Lord. The Bible says, "If we say that we have fellowship with Him, and walk in darkness, we lie and do not practice the truth" (1 John 1:6).

Someone wrote,

Buddha never claimed to be God.

Moses never claimed to be Jehovah.

Mohammed never claimed to be Allah.

Yet Jesus Christ claimed to be the true and living God.

Buddha simply said, "I am a teacher in search of the truth."

Jesus said, "I am the Truth."

Confucius said, "I never claimed to be holy."

Jesus said, "Who convicts me of sin?"

Mohammed said, "Unless God throws his cloak over me, I have no hope."

Jesus said, "Unless you believe in me, you will die in your sins."[63]

Many years ago, I visited an old monastery in India. I saw old relics that had been dug up and are now worshiped by Buddhists in the area. Muslims point with pride to Mecca, where the body of their prophet, Mohammed, is buried. Followers of Confucius revere the remains of their master, who is buried in an imposing tomb in Shandong, in the People's Republic of China. But what distinguishes Christianity from all other religions is the fact that Jesus lives and reigns as the only Savior of the world–His tomb empty.

What do Socrates, Bach, and Shakespeare have in common? They are remembered as bigger than life, but they are dead and in the grave and can do nothing for you. Walk into the great cathedrals whose spires pierce the sky, and you will see paintings and sculptures memorializing robust men who are still revered, and kind women who reach down to the lowly in compassion. But they, too, lie silent in death; they can do nothing for you.

But where is Jesus?

Sadly, artists too often have depicted Him as feeble, weak, and dead—still hanging on the cross. This is not the truth; for the One who is depicted hanging lifeless and broken on the cross is instead full of the breath of life, full of glory. He drank the cup of sin for all by emptying His life's blood so that He could fill us with the gift of eternal life by His resurrection.

Look to others and see that they are no different from you and me—we don't need a religion; we need a Savior. Christianity is the faith of the empty tomb, a religion centered not on a dead leader but on the living Lord.

PROOF COMES BY FAITH

While it is captivating to read what others say about Jesus Christ, faith is still the key to believing in Christ, who saves the sinner's soul.

As I meditate on the infallible proofs from Scripture of the life, death, and resurrection of this one solitary life, it occurs to me that there is a tremendous amount of convincing evidence—evidence that would be acceptable in any court of law as to the validity of Christ's resurrection.

But there are many who still have serious doubts. I am not presumptuous when I say that I have no doubts. I have experienced the living Christ in my heart. But for some of you who may be skeptical, there are many other reasons why I am sure that Christ rose from the dead.

Christ's birth was no ordinary birth.

It was accompanied by angels' voices and celestial wonders.

His life was no ordinary life, for it was marked by many signs and miracles.

We've seen that His death was no ordinary death, for it was distinguished by unusual compassion, geological disturbances, and solar irregularities.

Such a life could not long be contained in a grave, even though it was sealed in a prison of stone.

Yes, the Old Testament predicted that Christ would rise again. Every important event in Jesus' life was described many centuries before He came in the flesh, and when Jesus came, He fulfilled every prophecy.

"The Lord Himself will give you a sign: Behold, the virgin shall conceive and bear a Son, and shall call His name Immanuel" (Isa. 7:14). The Bible also says:

The Lord makes his life an offering for sin. . . . After he

has suffered, he will see the light of life. . . . He bore the sin of many, and made intercession for the transgressors. (Isa. 53:10–12 NIV)

We've also seen that during Christ's ministry He taught that He would die and be resurrected. This blessed Christ, who never deviated from the truth, can certainly be trusted, and His own words comprise the most reliable and convincing evidence of His resurrection.

Jesus connected His own resurrection with our endless life when He said, "I am the resurrection and the life. He who believes in Me, though he may die, he shall live. And whoever lives and believes in Me shall never die" (John 11:25–26).

Do you accept these words of Jesus? I do. Even His most avowed enemies never caught Him in a lie. He, who was truth itself, can be trusted implicitly.

He said He would be in the grave three days—and He was.

He said He would come forth from the grave—and He did.

He said that all those who believe in Him would have hope of everlasting life—and they have.

He said, "I am He who lives, and was dead, and behold, I am alive forevermore" (Rev. 1:18).

And we, also, will one day die and be resurrected. This is the great hope and certainty for those who follow Jesus.

We have the documented testimonies of those who were eyewitnesses to His resurrection. Angels, His disciples, the Roman soldiers, and a myriad of witnesses all shouted, "He is risen! Surely He is the Son of God."

The angel said to those who came to pay tribute to the dead, "Why do you look for the living among the dead? He is not here; he has risen! Remember how he told you, while he was still with you" (Luke 24:5–6 NIV). Mary Magdalene, scarlet sinner saved by grace, rushed breathlessly to the disheartened disciples with the glad news, "I have seen the Lord!" (John 20:18 NIV).

Peter, always the outspoken one, said, "We are witnesses of everything he did in the country of the Jews and in Jerusalem. They killed him by hanging him on a cross, but God raised him from the dead on the third day and caused him to be seen. . . . by us who ate and drank with him after he rose from the dead" (Acts 10:39–41 NIV).

Peter also wrote,

We did not follow cleverly devised stories when we told you about the coming of our Lord Jesus Christ in power, but we were eyewitnesses of his majesty. He received honor and glory from God the Father when the voice came to him from the Majestic Glory, saying, "This is my Son, whom I love; with him I am well pleased." We ourselves heard this voice that came from Heaven when we were with him on the sacred mountain. (2 Pet. 1:16–18 NIV)

The Bible says the apostle Paul "went into the synagogue, and on three Sabbath days he reasoned with them from the Scriptures, explaining and proving that the Messiah had to suffer and rise from the dead. 'This Jesus I am proclaiming to you is the [Christ],' he said" (Acts 17:2–3 NIV).

When you look for Jesus you will not find Him on the cross, nor will you find Him in the tomb—the cross is barren, the tomb empty. Your empty heart, though, can be filled with the forgiveness of the bloodstained cross and glory of the vacant tomb. He lives and abides within those who believe and obey Him by following His Word. We live and die, and in between we are all given the same choice— what will we do with Jesus—the resurrected Christ?

Even without these proofs I would still know that Christ lives because He lives in me. I talk to Him every morning when I wake up. He walks with me, and even as I write these words, His presence is overwhelmingly known. "For I am not ashamed of the gospel of Christ, for it is the power of God to salvation for everyone who believes" (Rom. 1:16).

Are you looking for Jesus? He is near you today.

Look at the cross, and you will see the evidence—His blood shed for you—but He is not there.

Look at the tomb, and you will see the evidence—it is empty—for He lives!

The Bible says, "Look to Me, and be saved. . . . For I am God, and there is no other" (Isa. 45:22).

Look for Jesus—He is knocking at the door of your heart.

Listen to God's promise to you: "But if the Spirit of Him who raised Jesus from the dead dwells in you, He who raised Christ from the dead will also give life to your mortal bodies through His Spirit who dwells in you" (Rom. 8:11). The evidence is before you. Examine it and then examine your heart. Roll back the stone of unbelief and behold the glow of an empty tomb and the thrill of a full heart and new life. The stone at Christ's tomb was not rolled away to let Jesus out but to let in the eyewitnesses to declare, "He is risen!"

James Hastings, a Scottish minister and biblical scholar in the early twentieth century, told an intriguing story about a German artist named Sternberg. As a little gypsy girl was sitting for a portrait in his studio, she noticed on the wall a half-finished portrait of Christ on the cross. The girl asked who it was. When told it was Jesus, she responded that He must have been a very wicked Man to have been nailed to a cross. The painter told her that, on the contrary, "Christ was the best man who ever lived, and He died on the cross that others might live." Then the little girl looked at him with such innocence and asked, "Did He die for you?" The question haunted Sternberg's conscience day and night, for though he knew the truth about Christ, he had not accepted Him as his Savior. He found he was no longer satisfied with life until he answered the question that you must also answer: Did He die for you?[64] If so, then you must die to self and find life anew in the resurrected Savior.

Have you received the living Christ? I am not asking you to receive a Christ who is hanging dead on a cross. Take Christ into your life—the resurrected Christ—who walks with those He has transformed by His grace. He lives and is coming back to earth someday.

Are you looking for Him? Has He changed your life? When you are asked "Where is Jesus?" I hope you can say with me, "He lives in my heart."

Seek the Lord while He may be found. Call upon Him while He is near. (Isa. 55:6) For the message of the cross . . . is the power of God. (1 Cor. 1:18)

CHAPTER 2

WHAT HAPPENED AT THE CROSS?

Through the death of Christ upon the cross, sin itself was crucified for those who believe in Him.

From New York's Fifth Avenue jewelry stores to the airport souvenir counters in Rome, Italy, one piece of jewelry is universally displayed—the cross.

What does the cross of Jesus mean? If we stopped people on the street to ask that question we might hear, "It's a symbol for Christianity, I guess." If we asked them "What happened at the cross?" Some might say "Jesus was a martyr and was nailed to the cross." Still others might say the cross was a myth. While most connect the emblem of the cross to religion, many do not understand its meaning.

Poet Thomas Victoria pictured Jesus on the cross, surrounded by men who were intent upon killing Him, and tried to express how Jesus might have spoken from the cross:

Oh, how sweet the wood of the cross,

How sweet the nails,

That I could die for you.

This deeply personal, intimate view of the cross is what the apostle Paul taught: that in the human experience it is a rare thing for one man to give his life for another, "yet the proof of God's amazing love is this: that it was while we were sinners that Christ died for us" (Rom. 5:8, PHILLIPS).

The focus of Paul's ministry to the great commercial city of Corinth was summed up when he said, "For I determined not to know anything among you except Jesus Christ and Him crucified" (1 Cor. 2:2).

But the average person in Corinth would have answered a question about the cross in the same way as the man on the street in the USA or any European, African, or Asian country. They lived in a city which was known for its depraved moral character. It was the kind of town in which we wouldn't want to raise our families.

The Corinthians were a sophisticated, sexually dissolute bunch, who thought that the cross was ridiculous, foolish, and even idiotic. Commenting on this view, Paul said, "The foolishness of God is wiser than men, and the weakness of God is stronger than men" (1 Cor. 1:25).

The preaching of the cross of Christ was a stumbling block to the Jews and idiocy to the philosophic Greeks. The philosophers believed they could unravel divine mysteries because they were overconfident of their own mental capacities. However, Paul said that the natural man (meaning the man who does not have the Spirit of God indwelling him) cannot understand the things of God. He meant that sin has twisted our understanding of truth so that we cannot recognize the truth about God.

Before the teaching in the Bible about the cross can mean anything to us, the Spirit of God must open our minds. The Scriptures teach that a veil covers our minds as a result of our separation from God.

To an "outsider," the cross must appear to be ridiculous. But to those who have experienced its transforming power, it has become the only remedy for the ills of each person, and of the world.

In spite of this available power, the gospel about Christ who was crucified is still unimportant to millions. They reflect the failure Paul analyzed when he questioned, "What have the philosopher, the writer and the critic of this world to show for all their wisdom? Has not God made the wisdom of this world look foolish? For it was after the world in its wisdom had failed to know God, that he in his wisdom chose to save all who believe by the 'simple-mindedness' of the Gospel message" (1 Cor. 1:20–21, PHILLIPS).

How can we brand the message of the cross as foolishness? Have we done so well with our private lives, with our families, and with our society that we can claim wisdom?

It's time we abandoned the pretense of being intellectual and recognize that our best minds are baffled by life.

God successfully changes men and women by the message that centers in the cross. We must recognize the disease of sin and claim God's healing ointment—forgiveness.

Daily, we profit from many helps beyond our understanding. We turn the faucet on seldom thinking of the water source or how it is carried through the pipes. We may not decipher a doctor's prescription, but we pay a high cost to fill it because we trust our physician.

In the same way we may be unable to fully comprehend the deep significance of the cross, but we can benefit from it because the Bible tells us what Christ accomplished on the cross to give us hope and assurance of eternal life.

The cross is the focal point in the life and ministry of Jesus Christ. Some think that God didn't want Christ to die but was forced to adjust His plans to adapt to it. Scripture makes it very clear, however, that the cross was no afterthought with God. Christ was delivered over by the predetermined plan and foreknowledge of God (Acts 2:23), and Jesus was perfectly obedient.

God designed the cross to defeat Satan, who by deception had obtained squatters' rights to the title deed of the world. Had Satan not set himself in opposition of God there would have been no need for God to send His Son to the cross, to die for the sins of the world.

When Satan with all of his clever promises separated man from God in the Garden of Eden, he did more than deceive Adam and Eve. In some mysterious manner he began to exert a kind of pseudo-sovereignty over man. In his arrogant violence, Satan unleashed his fiercest attack to halt Christ's ministry by putting into the hearts of the people to demand His death. But Satan was caught in his own trap; he couldn't comprehend that God so loved the world that He sent His only son to be the sin-bearer for man's sin.

So, what happened at the cross? The Bible says: "The Son of God appeared for this purpose, to destroy the works of the devil" (1 John 3:8 NASB). Only God can thwart the plans of Satan.

What a blow was dealt to Satan! Although he is still a wily pretender, his destruction was made certain by the victory of Christ at the cross. "That through death He might render powerless him who had the power of death, that is, the devil" (Heb. 2:14). What seemed to be the biggest defeat of history turned into the greatest triumph.

God not only overpowered Satan and conquered the

cross; Christ rescued those who Satan held captive and reconciled them to Himself. The Bible describes this divine plan: "We speak the wisdom of God in a mystery, the hidden wisdom which God ordained before the ages for our glory, which none of the rulers of this age knew, for had they known, they would not have crucified the Lord of glory" (1 Cor. 2:7–8).

If it were possible for one man, Adam, to lead mankind to ruin, why shouldn't it be possible for one man to redeem it? The Bible says, "For as in Adam all die, so also in Christ all will be made alive" (1 Cor. 15:22).

WHAT DID THE CROSS COST GOD?

People are filled with hurts, desires, and emotions, finding it almost impossible to stretch the mind to conceive what price Jesus paid to go to the cross and endure such agony. If He could have forgiven our sins by any other method, if the problems of the world could have been solved in any other way, God would not have allowed Jesus to die.

In the Garden of Gethsemane on the night before He was killed, Jesus prayed, "My Father, if it is possible, let this cup pass from Me." In other words, if there is any other way to redeem the human race, O God, find it! There was no other way. And then He prayed, "Not as I will, but as You will" (Matt. 26:39).

It is important to understand that when Jesus agonized that night in prayer, He was not just considering the act of dying. Just as His life was unique, so was His death. What happened to Him when He died never happened to any other person in the past and would never happen to anyone in the future.

To understand this, we need to look into God's revelation before Christ's earthly ministry, which brings us back to the Old Testament.

The orthodox Jewish religion was founded on God's grace. God entered into a covenant relationship with Israel, declaring Himself to be their God and stating in a special way that they were to be His people (Deut. 7:6). With this type of relationship, how were they to express their love for Him? The answer was by doing His will as it was described in the Old Testament law. But the people could not keep the law perfectly, and when they broke it, they sinned. As the Bible says, "Sin is the transgression of the law" (1 John 3:4 KJV).

The sacrifices in the temple were meant by God to show graphically that a person's guilt and penalty for sin could be transferred to another, and we see this in the symbolic sacrifice of a perfect animal bearing the penalty of sin through the shedding of blood.

Why did God give the law if He knew people couldn't possibly keep it? The Bible teaches that the law was given as a mirror. When we look into God's Word, we see what true righteousness is. The Ten Commandments describe the life that pleases God. If we are separated from God by sin, the law exposes our sin and shows us our true spiritual condition. Such a mirror does not reveal a very attractive image!

Sin had to be paid for, so in the beginning God instituted the sacrificial system by which we finally could be brought into a right relationship with God. In Old Testament times, those who had sinned brought sacrifices of animals and offered them to God. This foreshadowed the Great Sacrifice yet to come.

This is described by Moses in Leviticus 4. Man commits sin and wants God's forgiveness. He brings an animal, a perfect specimen, to the priest and lays his hand on its head. Symbolically, at that point the guilt and punishment he bears because of his sin pass to the animal. He then kills it as a sin offering, and the priest places some of the blood on the altar.

What is the significance? It is an atonement for the man in regard to his sin. In place of a broken relationship between God and the sinner, atonement results and he is forgiven by God.

The sacrifices were visual aids to show sinners that there was hope because the punishment for sin could be transferred to another. However, they were only symbols, because "It is not possible that the blood of bulls and goats could take away sins" (Heb. 10:4). But God could forgive them in the light of what He would one day do at the cross. Jesus, "after He had offered one sacrifice for sins forever, sat down at the right hand of God" (Heb. 10:12).

God did not initiate the sacrifices because He was bloodthirsty or unjust. He wanted us to zero in on two things: first, the loathsomeness of sin, and second, the cross on which God Himself would satisfy forever the demands of His justice. "Not with the blood of goats and calves, but with His own blood He entered the Most Holy Place once for all, having obtained eternal redemption" (Heb. 9:12).

When Christ atoned for sin, He stood in the place of guilty men and women. This is what happened at the cross.

If God had forgiven sin by a divine decree, issuing some sort of a heavenly document written across the sky, without the atonement which involved the personal shame, agony, suffering, and death of Christ, then we might assume that God was indifferent to sin. Consequently, we would all go on sinning, and the earth would become a living Hell.

In the suffering of Jesus, we have the participation of God in the act of atonement. Sin pierced God's heart.

God felt every searing nail and spear.

God felt the burning sun.

God felt the scorn of His tormenters and the body blows.

In the cross is the suffering love of God, bearing the guilt of man's sin. This love alone is able to melt the sinner's heart and bring him to repentance for salvation. "He [God the Father] made Him [Jesus] who knew no sin to be sin for us" (2 Cor. 5:21).

THE REASON FOR COMMUNION

The Bible tells us to "remember" these truths, and this is emphasized when people come to worship the Lord through communion (the Lord's Supper). Many, however, do not understand that this act of obedient worship centers on the cross and what happened there.

Jesus likens Himself to the Lamb that was offered as the sacrifice for atonement of sin and said to His disciples, "This is My body which is broken for you" (1 Cor. 11:24). When the cup is received, the emphasis is upon the fact that His blood is shed for the remission of sins. The elements of bread and the cup convey to us the reality of atonement and forgiveness. We can touch them, taste them, and see them. We have bread in our hand, but we have Christ in our hearts. We have the cup in our hand, but our souls experience Christ's forgiveness through His blood.

One of the most famous Scottish theologians was John Duncan of New College in Edinburgh. The story is told of communion being held in a Church of Scotland on one occasion. When the elements came to a sixteen-year-old girl, she turned her head aside and motioned for the elder to take the cup away—she couldn't drink it. John Duncan reached his long arm over, touched her shoulder, and said tenderly, "Take it, lassie, it's for sinners!"

Communion is for repentant sinners to remember what happened at the cross, for the work of man's redemption was accomplished there.

HOW CAN I UNDERSTAND ALL THIS?

It has been said that there was a cross in the heart of God long before the cross was erected at Calvary. The depths of God's love in sending His Son to pay such an awful price is beyond the measure of the human mind. But we must accept it on faith, or we will continually bear the burdens of guilt. We must accept the atonement that Christ has made and not try to make our own atonement; for this we can never do. Salvation is by Christ alone, through faith alone, and for the glory of God alone.

This is precisely what happened at the cross. Christ took the punishment which was due us. More than two thousand years ago God invited a morally corrupt world to the foot of the cross. There, God held your sins and mine to the flames until every last vestige of our guilt was consumed.

The greatest vision of sin that a person can ever receive is to look at what happened when Jesus died on the cross and rose again to new life. It is there that Christ paid the greatest debt mankind will ever incur, and it is through Jesus' sacrifice on the cross that everyone is given the freedom to receive God's greatest gift—the way of salvation—the hope of eternal life with Him.

Jesus did not willingly go to the cross so we could have an easy life. Someone has said, "Salvation is free, but not cheap." It cost Jesus His life. He died for you; will you live for Him?

Jesus said, "And he who does not take his cross and follow after Me is not worthy of Me. (Matt. 10:38)

CHAPTER 3

WHY JESUS SUFFERED

The cross demonstrates the suffering love of God.

Jesus suffered on the cross more than any other person in human history. The details of how He suffered were predicted in the prophecies of the Old Testament some five hundred to a thousand years before these events occurred. Yet He came down from Heaven and suffered with man all the way to the cross.

God is not blind. He knows about you, and He knows your pain. Our sufferings may be hard to bear, but they teach us important lessons, and we must learn to put our every care into His hands, for He helps us carry our cross of suffering.

There is self-denial when bearing a cross. We see it every day in heart-wrenching but heartwarming stories like the loving mother who saved her little daughter from a burning house. It left the young mother with severe burns on her hands and arms. When the girl grew up, not knowing how her mother's arms became so seared, she was ashamed of her mother's scarred and gnarled hands and always insisted that her mother wear long gloves to cover the ugliness.

But one day the grown child asked her mother how her hands became so scarred. For the first time the mother told how she had saved her daughter's life. The young woman wept tears of gratitude and said, "Oh Mother, those are beautiful hands, the most beautiful in the world. Don't ever hide them again."

Bearing a cross does not mean wearing a long face.

GOD JOINED US

God did not exclude Himself from human suffering. He became man—the Person of Christ—and shared with us all there is to share. Philip Yancey wrote, "God does not, in the comfortable surroundings of Heaven, turn a deaf ear to the sounds of suffering on this groaning planet."[1]

I have read stories, seen many paintings, and sat through numerous Christmas pageants about the birth of Jesus. It never ceases to stir me.

Jesus' life was in peril from His first cry. The most illustrious child ever born was hated by many while He lay in a manger, helpless to defend Himself.

We don't know much about His life as a child, but we do know that He lived with the knowledge of His destiny. His entire life was one of humility. He came not as a conquering king, which is what the Jews expected, but as a humble servant.

When He was an adult, the leaders were suspicious of this carpenter from Nazareth, because He was a threat to them. They scorned Him and treated Him with contempt. They said He broke God's law, that He was an unholy person, a drunkard, and one who made friends with the scum of society. He had the label of guilt-by-association stamped upon Him by self-righteous men.

Many people reacted violently to Him. At the beginning of His ministry, His own townsfolk at Nazareth tried to throw Him off a cliff (Luke 4:29). Religious and political leaders often conspired to seize and kill Him. And yet He healed the sick, fed the hungry, loved the unloved, taught the ignorant, and worked miracles among the multitudes. Ultimately, He was arrested and brought to trial before Pilate and Herod. Though innocent, He was denounced as an enemy of God and man. The frenzied mob incited the religious leaders and cried, "Crucify Him!"

THE CROSS: SYMBOL OF SUFFERING

Jesus knew in advance of going to the cross what was coming, and this increased His suffering. He knew the path to Calvary's cross would be painful. He foresaw the baptism of blood that awaited Him. He told His disciples very plainly about His coming death by crucifixion, which they could not understand at the time. And when the awful day came, they deserted Him.

We know what it means to have a friend come to us when we are in trouble. We long for someone to understand, to be with us, to hold us close and say, "I'm here to help." But when Jesus was arrested, His friends left Him.

What a devastation! At the end of training the twelve, they failed Him miserably. Anyone who has been deserted knows the terrible feeling of abandonment. Jesus appeared before His accusers and faced His trial without an earthly friend.

His trial led to a religious lynching. False witnesses accused Him with false evidence so that they could put Him to death, "but found none" (Matt. 26:59–60).

Still, the Jewish authorities were determined to have Him killed. Because Jews, under Roman rule, did not have the right to carry out the death penalty, they sought the permission of Pilate, the man appointed by Rome as overseer in Jerusalem. Pilate was convinced that Jesus was not guilty; three times he pronounced Him innocent. An idea came to him that he thought would absolve him of making a decision. It was his custom to release one prisoner at the time of Passover. "Do you want me to release to you the King of the Jews?" he asked, but they shouted back, "Not this Man, but Barabbas!" (John 18:39–40).

Pilate was disappointed with the crowd's choice to release Barabbas, a common criminal, instead of Jesus. He must have cringed when he saw the pitiful, bruised, and bleeding Jesus before the crowd. Instead of sympathy, he heard the shouts, "Crucify! Crucify!"

Pilate was a weak man, and when the chief priests told him that he would be Caesar's enemy if he did not kill this revolutionary, he gave in. Before he handed Jesus over to be crucified, he called for a basin and said, "I am innocent of this man's blood. It is your responsibility." He washed his hands of the whole affair. But this was no surprise to Jesus, for He had come for this very purpose. "This is the message which we have heard from Him . . . the blood of Jesus Christ His Son cleanses us from all sin" (1 John 1:5, 7).

THE CROSS AND THE
CLEANSING BLOOD

The mention of blood to many is gruesome. But the Bible says that the life of the flesh is in the blood (Lev. 17:11). During a visit to the Mayo Clinic I noticed on each reception desk a rack of pamphlets entitled *A Gift of Life,* urging people to donate to the blood bank. Anyone who has gone through surgery and looked up to see the bag of blood dripping slowly into their veins realizes with gratitude the life-giving property of the blood.

The message of the blood, the cross, and the work of redemption is "foolishness" to those who are perishing but "to us who are being saved, it is the power of God" (1 Cor. 1:18).

Jesus shed His blood for you—for me—that we might have life eternal and peace in the midst of storms. "Peace I leave with you; My peace I give to you; not as the world gives do I give you. Let not your heart be troubled, neither let it be afraid" (John 14:27).

God understands our pain. When tragedy strikes and suffering comes, we are faced with the all-important decision: Will we turn away from God, or will we turn toward Him? One day all suffering will end, and Satan will be banished. All the strife and hatred that twists and scars the world will vanish.

The greatest testimony to this dark world today is a band of crucified and risen men and women, dead to sin and alive unto God, bearing in their bodies "the marks of the Lord Jesus."

But God forbid that I should boast except in the cross of our Lord Jesus Christ . . . I bear in my body the marks of the Lord Jesus. (Gal. 6:14, 17 NKJV)

CHAPTER 4

PRICE OF VICTORY

The Bible tells us how to endure the storms of life and come through them with great victory. We will never know peace with God until we stand at the foot of the cross and identify with Christ through faith in Him.

The award-winning coach at the University of Alabama, Paul "Bear" Bryant, once said, "The price of victory is high but so are the rewards."[1] Another Paul, the great apostle, declared that he would not boast in anything except the cross of Jesus and said, "I press toward the goal for the prize of the upward call of God in Christ Jesus" (Phil. 3:14).

Victory is something we all want to experience. In fact, I have never met anyone who would choose defeat over victory. But through life we all experience both, whether a competition, or battle between our will and God's will.

What is the greatest and most costly battle ever to take place? Who was the victor, and what was the reward?

The greatest battle ever fought was between good and evil, and it took place at Golgotha, a rugged hill outside the walled city of Jerusalem. Jesus Christ was Victor, paying the cost with His blood. The reward was the salvation of human souls.

Jesus had spent three years with His disciples. He had walked with them across the plains and through the valleys.

He had sailed with them upon the waters. He had sat with them on the mountains and taught them many things, including this: "The Son of Man will be betrayed to the chief priests and to the scribes; and they will condemn Him to death, and deliver Him to the Gentiles to mock and to scourge and to crucify. And the third day He will rise again" (Matt. 20:18–19).

Jesus gave them a glimpse of what was to happen, but they did not comprehend that the Man they believed to be their King could ever fall into the brutal hands of mere men. They were focused on the Friend they called Master—the One who preached salvation and a coming kingdom, the One whom they believed to be the promised Messiah.

VICTORY FROM BONDAGE

Passover in the city of Jerusalem was a day of remembrance— the holiest of days for the Jews. This day marked victory from generations of bondage, freedom from enslavement by the Egyptian kingdom. What the Jewish nation failed to realize, however, was it had exchanged physical enslavement in Egypt for religious ritual as well as Roman rule.

Celebration of Passover for them was a time to remember God's intervention on their behalf to free them from their oppressors.

Jesus had been sent from Heaven to earth to identify with their suffering and to preach that His kingdom was not a human kingdom but the kingdom of God. He preached not religion but a personal relationship that God desired to have with people. They failed to see that God's law revealed humanity's sin. They didn't like to think of themselves as sinners. Pride in their religious heritage had blinded their eyes to the truth that they, too, were sinners in need of forgiveness. They continued the practice of the law and sacrifices offered for sins, unwilling to believe that Jesus had come to fulfill the law (Matt. 5:17) by cleansing it with His blood.

Many who followed Jesus loved the miracles that He performed. They loved His message of peace and love. But while they continued their sacrifices, they rejected the idea that their Messiah would have to offer Himself as the ultimate sacrifice for sin. They had missed the purpose of the sacrificial system, of slaying an innocent and unblemished lamb whose blood would cover sin that, for centuries, had pointed toward the cross. From the beginning this foreshadowed "the Lamb of God who takes away the sin of the world" (John 1:29). The Bible says, "These are a shadow of the things that were to come; the reality, however, is found in Christ" (Col. 2:17 NIV). But when Jesus spoke of His death and the cross, many turned away from Him, rejecting the truth that all men and women are sinners and must repent of their sins and follow Him by faith.

RESOUNDING VICTORY

As Passover approached that year, "all the chief priests and elders of the people plotted against Jesus to put Him to death" (Matt. 27:1). This brewing storm overshadowed the celebration that was taking place in the city. Jerusalem was the destination for travelers who had come to observe the most religious holiday in the land. It was to be a time of remembrance, proclaiming that they were the people of God. Instead they became a mob who cried out for the blood of God's Son—the very One who had come to redeem them from the bondage of sin and the law they could not keep.

No one there that day would ever have thought such chaos would result in resounding victory. How could such a cataclysmic event as the crucifixion of Jesus Christ, robed in horror and brutality, turn out victorious, pointing to the day when the King of kings would return robed in His glory? One must look into the Bible to find the truth.

People had turned the Feast of the Passover into a furious exhibition. Can you imagine a carnival-like atmosphere, seeing a crowd gathered to watch someone be tortured to death? To most in the modern world, this would be unthinkable. But this is the picture we see—a hostile crowd chanting for death. The people entertained themselves by demanding an innocent Man's murder while calling for a convicted prisoner's freedom.

This was no surprise to Jesus. He had told His disciples that He must die. He also told them that He would be victorious over death and the cross. But His words had been hard for them to comprehend.

The religious rulers had sought to find fault with Jesus. They demanded His death from the rulers of Rome. To keep peace in the city, Rome caved to the pressure of the Jews and sentenced Jesus to a Roman-style execution—on a cross.

THE OLD RUGGED CROSS

Some hang gold crosses around their necks. Others admire such a symbol mounted on a majestic cathedral. Some kneel by a cross of flowers plunged into the dirt at a loved one's gravesite. But on Passover that day the masses swarmed a pathway that led from the city gate, following the innocent Man bearing an old rugged cross, a symbol of agony, an instrument of shame. And it was a scandalous cross that Jesus bore for you and for me, all because of His amazing love.

The Bible tells us that after being ruthlessly beaten, Jesus was handed over to soldiers who laid a cross upon His flesh-torn back. Jesus wore the heaviness of man's sin upon His shoulders. He bore in His heart the ache for lost souls. He agonized under the tremendous weight as He ascended Golgotha's hill.

The people had not believed Jesus when He had said, "I am the way" (John 14:6). Yet they followed and pressed in on Him, mocking and ridiculing. The crowd had dismissed the truth when He had proclaimed, "I am . . . the truth." And as Truth climbed the craggy mountain, the people cried, "Crucify Him, crucify Him!" (Luke 23:21).

They had been victorious in their demands that Pilate end the life of the Man who came to give life. They had not believed Jesus when He had said, "I am . . . the life." And their taunting grew louder: "Crucify Him, crucify Him!"

Jesus stumbled beneath the tree upon which He would die for the sins of even those who falsely accused Him and mercilessly condemned Him to death. This instrument of death—the cross—would become a stumbling block to the rebellious and the mercy seat for the redeemed. Forgiveness and mercy for sinners—you and me—is what Jesus delivered from the cross. That is the victory of the cross.

Imagine the scene. Throngs of people were milling about, shouting over the gruesome sound of a mallet pounding spikes through the hands that had brought healing and feet that had walked on water. Some of the people gawking that day had perhaps witnessed His miracles; nearly all had heard of the great things He had done.

The cross of Jesus was hoisted up and plunged into the ground—the place of His crucifixion. The jolt would have caused unimaginable anguish. Jesus was raised up as a spectacle before violent spectators. There He hung in shame and reproach. On this most holy day, when no work was to be done or business transacted, man's most unholy work was done.

But Jesus had told His followers to expect this. "'And I, if I am lifted up from the earth, will draw all peoples to Myself.' This He said, signifying by what death He would die" (John 12:32–33). The weight of His body ripped away His flesh from the stakes thrust through Him. His very blood was poured out, staining the wood. His heart labored to beat as He looked down upon human hearts filled with sin.

NAILED TO THE CROSS

What did Jesus see from the cross? Mockers. His penetrating eyes looked into eyes blinded to the truth. He saw the religious leaders gaping at Him as they read the title nailed above His head, with the charge against Him written in three languages: "This is Jesus, the King of the Jews" (Matt. 27:37).

Intended to mock Jesus, the sign actually proclaimed the greatest truth: Jesus died for all.

The title was written in Hebrew so the religious would understand.

It was written in Greek so the cultured could understand.

It was written in Latin so world government could understand.

The message of the cross is for everyone. "For God did not send His Son into the world to condemn the world, but that the world through Him might be saved" (John 3:17). The cross shows the seriousness of our sin, but it also proclaims the immeasurable love of God. Jesus says to the human race, "I will meet you at only one place, and that is the cross—the place of victory."

THE FOOT OF THE CROSS

Jesus looked at the crowd gathered, but most of His followers had fled. His disciples, except John, had deserted Him. The only solemn presence was found in the agonized faces and shattered hearts of Jesus' mother, some other women, and a few friends who stood watching in horror.

Jesus watched as the Roman guards gambled for His garments at the foot of the cross. No doubt during their rowdy game, they glanced up toward the Heavens, watching Jesus, whom they had flogged, bleeding and gasping for breath in the heat of day. The Bible says, "Sitting down, they kept watch over Him there" (Matt. 27:36).

On either side of Jesus hung two criminals—thieves and

murderers—who in spite of their own pain found strength to slander Him. One said, "If You are the Christ, save Yourself and us" (Luke 23:39). Others who passed by hurled insults at Him, saying, "Save Yourself! If You are the Son of God, come down from the cross" (Matt. 27:40).

The chief priests, teachers of the law, and the elders sneered, "He saved others; Himself He cannot save. Let the Christ, the King of Israel, descend now from the cross that we may see and believe" (Mark 15:31–32). The soldiers also mocked him and said, "If You are the King of the Jews, save Yourself" (Luke 23:37). They puffed themselves up as they carried out the gore and shame of crucifying an innocent Man.

This wasn't a somber scene where people comforted the dying. This was a scandalous scheme, where bloodthirsty people gathered to falsely accuse the very One who represented eternal life. Hatred and hostility permeated the atmosphere. The crowd delighted in jeering Him who had come to save them from evil. This is what Jesus saw and heard from the cross. He saw the wickedness of the people's hearts. He heard the vile reproach from their lips.

You may rightly say, "This is not a picture of victory."

It is only when we hear the words that came from His

lips that we can rejoice in what it all meant that day, and what it still means today.

What did the Master say to the soldiers who tortured Him?

What did the Son of God say to His Father who had forsaken Him?

What did Jesus say to His mother who grieved?

What did the King of the Jews say to the religious leaders who called out to Him?

What did the Son of Man say to those who taunted Him?

From the same lips that spoke peace during His three-year ministry, Jesus spoke love to His friends as well as His enemies.

THE MESSAGE FROM THE CROSS

Jesus willingly died on the cross to identify with all those searching for truth. Are you among them? Have you heard what Jesus has said to you from the cross? You were there. I was there. Oh, it's true that we hadn't been born yet, but our sins were present that day. It wasn't just the soldiers, thieves, religious leaders, and passersby who took part in the crucifixion of Jesus Christ. Our sins also nailed Him to the tree.

No one could have forced Jesus to the cross had He been unwilling to go. This is the crux of the cross—Jesus chose to go to Calvary. He willingly laid down His life for the sins of the world. He died of His own volition by allowing your sins and my sins to be nailed to His cross.

The Bible says that we are doomed to eternal banishment from the presence of God because sin separates man from God. Remember, sin brings about a penalty: "The soul who sins shall die" (Ezek. 18:20). But Jesus Christ said, "I will die in their place. I'll take their judgment. I'll take their death. I'll go to the cross." This is what Christ did for you and for me. Two thousand years ago, God invited a morally corrupt world to the foot of the cross. When Jesus hung on the cross, a great unseen cosmic battle raged in the heavens. And, in the end, Christ triumphed over all the forces of evil and death and Hell, giving us the greatest of all hope— eternal forgiveness.

Though the cross repels, it also attracts. It possesses a magnetic quality. Once you have been to the cross, you will never be the same. The greatest vision of sin is at the cross, where we also see the greatest vision of love. "Greater love has no one than this, than to lay down one's life for his friends" (John 15:13). Jesus hung from the cross with us in mind. And as He hung there, He preached the most powerful sermon. In just seven brief phrases, He encapsulated the totality of His three-year ministry.

JESUS, THE GREAT FORGIVER

The first message Jesus preached from the cross was forgiveness.

Crucifixion is an evil death. The position of the victim on the cross results in asphyxia, prohibiting adequate exhalation and inhalation of air. Breathing is laborious and speaking insufferable. Yet in the midst of this agony, Jesus ministered to humanity's vilest and also to the brokenhearted. This is why the cross is often seen as the symbol of Christianity.

As the guards divided His garments by casting lots, Jesus said, "Father, forgive them, for they do not know what they do" (Luke 23:34). Even from the cross, Jesus spoke to His Heavenly Father on behalf of His enemies. This was a message Jesus' followers had struggled with: "But I say to you, love your enemies, bless those who curse you, do good to those who hate you, and pray for those who spitefully use you and persecute you, that you may be sons of your Father in Heaven" (Matt. 5:44–45).

The cross throws a great searchlight on the evil of the world. We don't want the searchlight of the cross examining our hearts, telling us that we're guilty before God.

The blood of Jesus convicts, but it also cleanses.

The blood of Jesus brings reproach, but it also brings redemption.

The blood of Jesus frustrates evil, but it also brings forgiveness to the sinner.

The blood of Jesus cancels God's judgment on the repentant heart.

JESUS, THE GREATER SAVIOR

The second message Jesus preached was of salvation and assurance. As Jesus emptied out His life's blood, He heard the thieves on either side of Him debating what they had heard about the Christ.

One rejected salvation with sarcasm. But the other received Him.

The one who rejected Jesus blasphemed Him, saying, "If You are the Christ, save Yourself and us."

But the other rebuked him, saying, "Do you not even fear God, seeing you are under the same condemnation? And we indeed justly, for we receive the due reward of our deeds; but this Man has done nothing wrong." Then he said to Jesus, "Lord, remember me when You come into Your kingdom." And Jesus said to him, "Assuredly, I say to you, today you will be with Me in Paradise" (Luke 23:39–43).

Jesus knew the hearts of these convicted criminals, but only one became convicted of his sin. The Bible says conviction leads to repentance. The thief, who no doubt also labored to speak, confessed his sins, admitting that his deeds deserved the punishment of death. He acknowledged that Jesus was innocent of all wrongdoing. And by asking to be received in Jesus' kingdom, he proclaimed that Jesus truly was the King.

The Bible says, "The word is near you, in your mouth and in your heart" (that is, the word of faith which we preach): that if you confess with your mouth the Lord Jesus and believe in your heart that God has raised Him from the dead, you will be saved. For with the heart one believes unto righteousness, and with the mouth confession is made unto salvation. For the Scripture says, "Whoever believes on Him will not be put to shame. For there is no distinction between Jew and Greek, for the same Lord over all is rich to all who call upon Him." (Rom. 10:8–12)

The thief displayed this remarkable faith. He was hanging near the cross of Christ, and the very Word—the Lord Jesus—was near him, receiving his repentant heart.

The only deathbed repentance in the whole Bible is this account of the thief on the cross. I have known a few people who accepted Christ as their Savior just before drawing their last breath. But my friend, do not presume on the grace of God, for the Scripture says, "Now is the accepted time; behold, now is the day of salvation" (2 Cor. 6:2).

Nowhere in Scripture are we promised tomorrow. The Scripture doesn't say that tomorrow is the day of salvation, for that would tempt us to continue in sin for another day. Do you understand the urgency and necessity of salvation? The thief understood it more than being bound to the cross of death; he was at the crossroads of decision. He chose the only path to salvation, for salvation comes only through the cross of Christ. Christ is the way, His word is the truth, and His death and resurrection bring life.

There weren't many that day thinking of the promised resurrection. But the words of the thief revealed his faith in that glorious hope. In the midst of suffering, surrounded by vile men, Jesus was pleased to hear the sincere words of repentance, "Lord, remember me when You come into Your kingdom."

This sinner hanging near the cross of Jesus found salvation that very hour. In his letter to the Romans, Paul quoted from the Old Testament:

Whoever calls on the name of the LORD

Shall be saved. (Joel 2:32)

The thief would never have the opportunity to walk in the ways of Christ on earth, but for more than two thousand years his testimony of what Jesus Christ did for him has spoken from the pages of Scripture—just as the psalm foretold:

Future generations will be told about the Lord. They will proclaim his righteous, declaring to a people yet unborn: He has done it! (Psa. 22:30–31 NIV)

The Savior willingly poured out His blood for the sin of humanity, knowing that "without the shedding of blood there is no forgiveness of sins" (Heb. 9:22 ESV). This criminal-turned-convert exhibited faith beyond reason.

Faith means that you totally commit to Christ. Your hope is in Him alone. He becomes the One in whom you trust completely for your salvation. The Scripture says, "So then faith comes by hearing, and hearing by the word of God" (Rom. 10:17).

We see the contrast between these two criminals and their responses to Jesus. Both saw Him unjustly condemned. Both heard His message from the cross. Jesus looked into the hearts of these two men just as He sees into our hearts today. His arms were stretched out as if to say, "Come."

His ears were not dull. He heard the insults of rejection, and He heard the faint plea of repentance:

Behold, the LORD's hand is not shortened,

That it cannot save;

Nor His ear heavy,

That it cannot hear. (Isa. 59:1)

There are two classes of people in the world: the saved and the lost. Both have the same opportunity to choose Christ or reject Him. These two criminals represent all human beings, all having the same choice. The one who rejected Christ cursed Him while the other confessed Him. The latter knew he deserved death, but in his own weakness he exhibited the faith to believe that Jesus Christ was indeed the Savior of the world. The Bible says, "For indeed the gospel was preached to us as well as to them; but the word which they heard did not profit them, not being mixed with faith in those who heard it" (Heb. 4:2).

Repentance is by faith, believing that God will forgive. Repentance is acknowledging your sin and by faith, accepting Christ's forgiveness, changing your mind about who Jesus Christ is and what He has done for you, then turning from sin and going the way of the cross. When you do this, He empowers you to believe that He will cleanse you from sin and give you a new heart, a renewed mind, and the will to follow Him into His kingdom.

This convert had a change of attitude. As Jesus was finishing His work on the cross, this man was a few breaths from death, and he was promised a new beginning—eternal life in paradise—in the presence of God.

When we read the account of the crucifixion, it is easy to miss the glory of the cross because of its shame—shame for human sin that nailed Jesus to the tree. The cross represents the suffering love of God, which bears the guilt of humanity's sin, which alone is able to melt the sinner's heart and bring him to repentance for salvation. This is the glory of the cross.

JESUS, THE GREAT COMFORTER

The third message Jesus preached was that of comfort, despite the anguish He endured. The nails that pierced the hands and feet of Jesus were not nearly as painful as man's sin, which pierced the heart of Jesus. Yet the blood that flowed from Jesus' veins was as precious as the love that flowed from His heart to save the souls of many.

Jesus' flesh scorched in the blaze of the sun, yet He preached comfort as He had done so many times. Jesus set aside His own distress to care for and make provision for His mother. He knew that His disciples had deserted Him, yet when He looked down from the cross, He saw that one had returned to Mary's side: "When Jesus therefore saw His mother, and the disciple whom He loved standing by, He said to His mother, 'Woman, behold your son!' Then He said to the disciple, 'Behold your mother!' And from that hour that disciple [John] took her to his own home" (John 19:26–27).

The night before, Jesus had promised His disciples that He would not leave His own "comfortless" (John 14:18 KJV). Even from the cross of His suffering, we see Jesus nurturing relationships and giving hope. For this is precisely why He died: to bring mankind back into fellowship with His Father in Heaven.

We are told that "the Son of Man did not come to be served, but to serve, and to give His life a ransom for many" (Matt. 20:28). Jesus Himself had said this to His disciples, and on the cross, we see Jesus exemplifying His word of truth.

While Jesus was crucified by sinful people, His death was voluntary: "No one takes [My life] from Me, but I lay it down of Myself. I have power to lay it down, and I have power to take it again" (John 10:18). Jesus did so to fulfill the prophecy found in the book of Isaiah, written five hundred years earlier, that the Lamb of God would be led away to the slaughter:

He was despised and rejected by mankind, a man of suffering, and familiar with pain. . . . he was despised, and we held him in low esteem. Surely he took up our pain and bore our suffering, yet we considered him punished by God, stricken by him, and afflicted. But he was pierced for our transgressions, he was crushed for our iniquities; the punishment that brought us peace was on him, and by his wounds we are healed. . . . (Isa. 53:3–5 NIV)

Jesus today is seated at the right hand of His Father in Heaven, making intercession for those who belong to Him. His words are still bringing comfort to those who, like Mary, are overcome with despair, overwrought with pain, and overlooked by others. Jesus came to identify with us in all of these things and give hope.

The Bible says,

Because of the LORD's great love we are not consumed, for his compassions never fail. They are new every morning; great is *your* faithfulness. . . . The LORD is good to those whose hope is in him, to the one who seeks him; it is good to wait quietly for the salvation of the LORD. (Lam. 3:22–26 NIV)

It is impossible to imagine the ripping pain Mary must have felt as she watched her Son bleeding, suffering an agonizing death; heard His last words; and was helpless to comfort Him. Surely, if anyone could have the full assurance that Jesus' death would end in victory, it was Mary, for she knew beyond any doubt that Jesus had been conceived of the Holy Spirit. She knew beyond the shadow of the cross that Jesus the Son of God would live again.

JESUS, THE GREAT RECONCILER

The fourth message from the cross was one of reconciliation. Jesus, who knew no sin, had to deal with sin in order to reconcile man to God. In this darkest hour, reconciliation was victoriously won.

What must have gone through Mary's mind when she heard the wailing voices directed at Jesus? His accusers shouted, "Let God rescue him now if he wants him, for he said, 'I am the Son of God'" (Matt. 27:43 NIV). But Jesus did not come down from the cross. God the Father did not rescue Him. Why? Because Jesus willingly gave up His life to save others.

When Jesus' disciples refused the previous night to believe that He would be crucified on a cross, Jesus had said to them, "Now my soul is troubled, and what shall I say? 'Father, save me from this hour?' No, it was for this very reason I came to this hour. Father, glorify your name!" (John 12:27–28 NIV).

He could have called legions of angels to His side.

But He chose to die in order to spare us eternal death.

He chose to suffer to grant us comfort.

He chose to give up His earthly life that we might have everlasting life.

This is my hope. Is it yours?

Jesus suffered the persecution of His own people. He suffered desertion by His own disciples. But worse than all that, He suffered abandonment from His Father in Heaven for the glory of God. No wonder Jesus cried out from the cross, "My God, My God, why have You forsaken Me?" (Mark 15:34). God the Son had never been separated from God the Father, and Jesus felt the horrific pain of isolation as He endured God's wrath upon the evil of sin.

Eyes were blinded. Hearts were like stone. Ears were deaf to the truth. On the cross Jesus was severely afflicted with the sins of the world, but it was also on the cross that He completed the greatest of all of His works.

The cross is where sin met the Savior.

The cross is where the sinner finds salvation.

The cross is where wretched souls can find victory in Jesus.

Jesus endured grief that cannot be fathomed. This is the bloodstained picture of sin that separates men and women from fellowship with God. We must crucify—put to death— our ways and go the way of the cross. When we do that, we participate in His great work of reconciliation.

JESUS, THE GREAT THIRST QUENCHER

As Jesus' time was at hand, He preached the fifth message from the cross: "I thirst!" (John 19:28). Just imagine His parched lips, His blistering skin, every ligament, tendon, and muscle burning from being stretched out on a cruel cross. He had been whipped beyond recognition even before being nailed to the tree. In severe distress, He writhed from inflamed wounds, immense grief, and fatigue of body, soul, and spirit, culminating in nature's deepest need to quench insufferable thirst.

But the soldiers' hearts were hardened; they continued to antagonize. One of them dipped a sponge in wine vinegar and lifted it up on the stalk of the hyssop plant to Jesus. But I believe there was something Jesus thirsted for more; everything He did and said pointed to His passion to save lost souls. Jesus thirsted for souls.

This had been evident earlier in His ministry when He journeyed into Samaria. The Bible says in John 4 that it was late in the day—"About the sixth hour" (v. 6)—and Jesus was weary and thirsty. He sat down near Jacob's well, and a woman came to draw water. Jesus asked her for a drink . . .

but His aim was to speak to her about her soul. The woman was troubled by Jesus' request because she knew that Jews did not associate with Samaritans. "How is it that You, being a Jew, ask a drink from me, a Samaritan woman?" (v. 9). They conversed a bit more, and then Jesus told her something that changed her life: "Whoever drinks of this [well] water will thirst again, but whoever drinks of the water that I shall give him will never thirst. But the water that I shall give him will become in him a fountain of water springing up into everlasting life" (vv. 13–14).

Now we look at Jesus on the cross, at about the sixth hour, saying, "I thirst." The enemy lifted up sour vinegar, representing the sourness of sin. Jesus had taken the cup of sin's wrath, completing His earthly mission. In that moment He grappled with Hell, judgment, sin, and death; and He defeated them all. He had come to rescue and to save the lost. His accusers had intended the cross for harm, "but God intended it for good to accomplish what is now being done, the saving of many lives" (Gen. 50:20 NIV). And to do that, He had to die that we might live.

That is why I love to gaze at the cross. In it we see the expression of the greatest love of God for man. The Lord "turned the curse into a blessing for you, because the LORD your God loves you" (Deut. 23:5). Jesus, the Living Water, sustains and nourishes our weary souls.

JESUS, THE FURNISHER AND FINISHER OF OUR FAITH

The sixth message from the lips of Jesus was that His work on the cross was complete. He had satisfied the penalty for sin through His own death and had completed His rescue mission to redeem the souls of men. Now He could sound the victory cry: "It is finished!" (John 19:30).

What was finished? Certainly not Jesus' life, for He had told the disciples that He would die and be raised on the third day. It was the payment of sin that was finished—paid in full by the willing sacrifice of Jesus' own blood to redeem man's soul. "You were not redeemed with corruptible things . . . but with the precious blood of Christ, as of a lamb without blemish and without spot" (1 Pet. 1:18–19).

Jesus was not forced to lay down His life to pay for sin. He gave Himself as the substitutionary lamb, the Lamb of God slain for the world, just as the Bible says, and He is now the Shepherd of souls. "For you were like sheep going astray, but have now returned to the Shepherd and Overseer of your souls" (1 Pet. 2:25).

The Bible also says, "When he had received the drink, Jesus said, 'It is finished.' With that, he bowed his head and gave up his spirit" (John 19:30 NIV). On His own accord, He quietly, reverently, and deliberately bowed His head, knowing He had finished the work His Father had given Him to do.

"It is finished" is a proclamation of salvation's completed plan. Never again will blood be shed for sin. Jesus Christ has paid the ransom.

Had Jesus been rescued from the cross by His Father, the ransom for sin would have never been paid. For this profound reason, God had sent Jesus on a rescue mission to save the souls of mankind, and Jesus was obedient to the Father's calling. God the Father and God the Son are one, unified in bringing about the great gift of our salvation, our victory, found in Jesus Christ.

How mysteriously wonderful it is that Christ willingly took your place and mine. We now have the opportunity to finish with the hope and certainty of eternal life because of victory in the cross of Christ—"Looking unto Jesus, the author and finisher of our faith" (Heb. 12:2).

JESUS, THE GREAT VICTOR

In Scripture the number seven is symbolic of completion. Jesus began His seven-point sermon from the cross by calling on His Father, and He concluded this life-changing message in the Father's name. Most of those around Him paid no attention—until the sixth hour. Night had not fallen, but the sun stopped shining, and darkness covered the land. Jesus cried out with the voice of victory, "'Father, "into Your hands I commit My spirit."' Having said this, He breathed His last" (Luke 23:46).

Jesus, who had been delivered into the hands of sinners, was now in the hands of God the Father. Sin had been crucified once and for all.

At that moment, the Bible says, the curtain of the temple was torn in two from top to bottom. The earth shook, the rocks split and the tombs broke open. The bodies of many holy people who had died were raised to life. . . .

When the centurion and those with him who were guarding Jesus saw the earthquake and all that had happened, they were terrified, and exclaimed, "Surely he was the Son of God!" (Matt. 27:51–54 NIV)

And "when all the people who had gathered to witness

this sight saw what took place, they beat their breasts and went away" (Luke 23:48 NIV). For this moment in time the gamblers and the grumblers, the scoffers and the swindlers, were silenced. Their excruciating assault of Jesus was now their unrelenting nightmare.

YOU WERE THERE

With whom do you identify at the cross of Jesus Christ? Are you just passing by, scoffing at what Christ has done for you, or are you thirsting for the life that Jesus longs to give you? Do you identify with the thief who rejected Christ as Lord or the thief who repented to Jesus the Savior?

There are some who might identify with the religious rulers who believed they were holy and righteous, yet in vengeance they betrayed, mocked, and murdered the Righteous One.

Perhaps you see yourself sitting with the soldiers, gambling for a little piece of Jesus; or standing with Mary and John, waiting to be comforted by Jesus. Will you go down in defeat as the executioners did when they felt the power of the earthquake that knocked them to their knees, or will you say with the centurion, "Surely He was the Son of God!"?

Are you standing near the cross with a heart wrenched in pain as you consider the Savior who shed His blood for you?

Are you agonizing over your sins that nailed Jesus to the tree?

He agonized for you.

Are you willing to be persecuted for the name of Jesus?

He was persecuted for you. He suffered for you.

Will you commit your spirit into the hands of the One who died for you?

Jesus looked down from the cross on our sin and loved us in spite of it.

Will you look to Him and be saved (Isa. 45:22)?

The Bible says that Jesus "forgave us all our sins, having canceled the charge of our legal indebtedness, which stood against us and condemned us; he has taken it away, nailing it to the cross. And having disarmed the powers and authorities, he made a public spectacle of them, triumphing over them by the cross" (Col. 2:13–15 NIV).

Jesus defeated sin, and His victory over death brings life and hope to the souls of men. Scripture tells us that the sting of death is sin. "But thanks be to God, who gives us the victory through our Lord Jesus Christ" (1 Cor. 15:57).

The price of victory was the precious blood of Jesus, and

the reward is in the souls won for His Father's kingdom. Will you remain defeated by sin, or will you say, "I am finished with sin's hold on me and ready to take hold of Christ who has finished the work of redemption?"

The suffering cross of Jesus is stained with the sins of the world, but the glorious cross of Christ cleanses sinners' hearts stained by sin, and to all who are saved, it is a tree of life. For the Christian, death can be faced realistically and with victory through the cross of Jesus.

Whoever believes that

Jesus is the Christ is

born of God . . .

And this is the victory that

has overcome the world—

our faith. (1 John 5:1, 4)

CHAPTER 5

THE CROSS EVERLASTING

Jesus' greatest work was achieved in
three dark hours on the cross at Calvary;
the greatest victory is His resurrection
that points to life everlasting.

The Twin Towers at New York's World Trade Center collapsed as the world watched with horror on that terrible day in 2001 that has become known as 9/11. In the aftermath of the terror attack, a twenty-foot steel beam cross was uncovered. The sight of the cross brought hope to many—and terror to some. A firefighter said: "We thought the devil was here, but with this cross, we know God is here."[1]

When the World Trade Center Cross was later displayed, some demanded that the cross be removed from the privately operated 9/11 Memorial and Museum, claiming that many people were "injured" when they saw it.

To some the cross of Christ brings cheer; to others it incites fear. The cross can be of comfort to people's spirits, or it can reveal the corruption of the human heart and bring conviction of sin. This is an illustration of what the apostle Paul spoke of when he said, "But God forbid that I should boast except in the cross of our Lord Jesus Christ, by whom the world has been crucified to me, and I to the world" (Gal. 6:14).

Paul's message of the Gospel was centered on Jesus Christ and the cross that He bore for the whole world. Paul could have gloried in many things about himself. He was highly educated, a religious scholar and theologian of the Scripture, a Roman citizen with impeccable ancestry, and a skilled orator.

Paul could have also gloried in his encounter with the incarnate Christ on the Damascus Road and the healing of his blindness. He could have gloried in the healing powers he possessed. He could have even gloried in his call to preach to the Gentile world.

But instead Paul gloried in the cross. Why? Jesus' crucifixion on the cross was the most terrible of all deaths, but Paul understood what the cross represented, and that message fueled his resolve to go into the world and preach the Gospel of Christ. Paul understood the twofold message of the cross of Christ—God's judgment on sin and His great love for the sinner. Paul gloried in the duplicity of what the cross represented.

You see, the cross shows the depth of our sins. We cannot know how deeply sin offends God until we look at the cross. People today look at the cross as a symbol of forgiveness, without considering the sin that put Christ there. The cross, without its powerful message, is powerless.

WHAT SIN DOES

When you hang a beautiful cross around your neck or pin it on your lapel, remember that it is man's sin that sent Jesus Christ to the cross. Let it remind you of the tremendous gift that it brings, but never forget that it was because of our sin that Christ had to die there. And never underestimate the destructive power of sin:

Sin affects the mind. "The natural man does not receive the things of the Spirit of God . . . because they are spiritually discerned" (1 Cor. 2:14).

Sin affects the will. People easily become slaves to their sins. But Jesus said that His truth will set us free (John 8:32).

Sin affects the conscience. The Bible says, "And their conscience, being weak, is defiled" (1 Cor. 8:7).

WHY GLORY IN THE CROSS?

Paul gloried in the cross because it demonstrates God's judgment on sin through the willing sacrifice of Christ on behalf of sinful man.

We have turned, every one, to his own way; And the Lord has laid on Him the iniquity of us all. (Isa. 53:6)

But he also gloried in the cross because it shows the love of God. "For God so loved the world that He gave His only begotten Son" (John 3:16). But there are other reasons Paul gloried in the cross.

Paul gloried in the cross because it is the only way to salvation. "For there is no other name under Heaven given among men by which we must be saved" (Acts 4:12).

Paul gloried in the cross because it gave a new dynamic to life. "Old things have passed away; behold, all things have become new" (2 Cor. 5:17).

Paul gloried in the cross because he knew it guaranteed the future life. "God has given us eternal life, and this life is in His Son" (1 John 5:11).

Paul gloried in the cross because Christ defeated death by His resurrection. "Everyone who sees the Son and believes in Him may have everlasting life; and I will raise him up at the last day" (John 6:40).

WHAT THE CROSS REPRESENTS

The cross is the meeting place between God and man, and Jesus is the bridge. "For He Himself is our peace . . . and has broken down the middle wall of separation . . . that He might reconcile them both to God in one body through the cross" (Eph. 2:14–16).

The cross is also the symbol of forgiveness. "Father, forgive them, for they do not know what they do" (Luke 23:34).

The cross represents reconciliation. "But now in Christ Jesus you who once were far off have been brought near by the blood of Christ" (Eph. 2:13).

The cross represents God's peace. "For it pleased the Father that in Him all the fullness should dwell, and by Him to reconcile all things to Himself, by Him, whether things on earth or things in Heaven, having made peace through the blood of His cross" (Col. 1:19–20).

The cross represents victory over the flesh. "You once walked according to the course of this world . . . and were by nature children of wrath. . . . But God, who is rich in mercy, because of His great love . . . made us alive together with Christ" (Eph. 2:2–5).

THE WORK OF THE CROSS IS ETERNAL

Once you've been to the cross, you can never be the same, and you will never be ashamed of what Jesus Christ has done for you.

The work of Christ on the cross is eternal. Its glory will never fade. The cross was in the heart of the Father and the Son from the beginning, and the Lord did not leave the cross behind when He left this world. The cross is also in the hearts of those who have committed themselves to the Lord.

The tree of life was planted in the Garden long ago. It was not uprooted because of man's sin. No, man was uprooted—removed from the tree's life-giving power. Jesus came to restore the power by putting the cross into the hearts of people. That is why Jesus said, "If anyone desires to come after Me, let him . . . take up his cross, and follow Me" (Matt. 16:24).

The cross—His cross—is eternal in its judgment. Moreover, it is eternal by the love it sheds in the hearts of His people. This is why Paul said he would glory only in the cross. This is why he told us to sow to the Spirit that reaps everlasting life (Gal. 6:8).

We cannot just look at the cross as an emblem. The cross must bring us to a decision. Will we cling to it and carry it in our hearts, sowing its message of love and new life, or will we allow the life-giving message to be buried in the rubble of sin, bringing judgment? Will you reap the eternal life of glory, or eternal life bound in shame?

The eternal destination for believers in Christ is the glory of Heaven, provided by the glory of the cross of Him who died for the world. Do not cling to the well-polished cross on display. Cling to the old rugged cross that is blood-stained, for it is the way by which our sinful hearts are washed whiter than snow.

[Jesus] bore our sins in his body on the cross, so that we might die to sins and live for righteousness; by his wounds you have been healed. (1 Pet. 2:24 NIV)

CHAPTER 6

THE KING'S ETERNAL REIGN

Christ's kingdom is already being built up in the hearts of those who come to the foot of His cross, surrender to His lordship, and serve Him as King of kings who reigns from His eternal throne.

N o wonder He was a carpenter.

Cradled in a manger made of wood, He brought Christmas joy to the world at His birth.

He is Jesus.

Nailed to an old rugged cross and lifted up to die for sin, He brought Easter glory to the world by His resurrection.

He is the Savior.

Coming again as the Branch of righteousness, He will bring an everlasting kingdom and will reign in power.

Behold! His name is the Branch.

Why Branch? At the time of Jesus' birth, the royal line of David—from which He came—had dried up in Israel. But He would still be King, for *Branch* is a title for Messiah and speaks of fruitfulness. The prophet Isaiah said,

> There shall come forth a Rod from the stem of Jesse,
> And a Branch shall grow out of his roots. (Isa. 11:1)

When Jesus stepped down from His eternal throne, He came as Servant—the Vine of the Vinedresser—who brings life. The Child from Heaven had royal blood in His veins, though He was born in a stable. But when He comes back, "the Lord God will give Him the throne of His father David. And He will reign . . . forever, and of His kingdom there will be no end" (Luke 1:32–33).

This is why the prophet Zechariah prophesied that the Messiah would come from David's royal lineage and said, "Behold, the man whose name is The BRANCH!" (Zech. 6:12). No wonder the Branch will then say, "*I am* . . . your King" (Isa. 43:15).

It is hard to grasp that a King would serve, but this is no ordinary king. This is Jesus, whose Father proclaimed, "I am bringing forth My Servant the Branch."

He will be gloriously crowned. He will sit on His righteous throne and from His place He shall branch out—to serve. How will He serve? He will harvest His bounty—souls to fill Heaven.

THE TREES OF GOD

No wonder the Bible has a lot to say about roots, seeds, branches, and vines—and trees. I can't help but wonder what went through the mind of Jesus as He worked in the carpenter's shop, filled with varied woods harvested from the forests. We certainly know that He spoke of trees to illustrate truth as He walked the valleys and hills with His disciples. Nearly every biblical writer wrote about the trees.

Perhaps this is why Ezekiel described the coming kingdom this way: Trees of all kinds will grow along both sides of the river. The leaves of these trees will never turn brown and fall, and there will always be fruit on their branches.... They [will be] watered by the river flowing from the Temple. The fruit will be for food and the leaves for healing. (47:12 NLT)

This is certainly a picture of the coming King: from the root of Jesse, from the seed of David, whose name is Branch. No wonder Jesus called Himself the true Vine—"I *am* the vine; you are the branches" (John 15:5)—for eternal life flows from the vine to the branches. This is Heaven's family tree.

No wonder Jesus found strength as He kneeled among the olive trees in the Garden of Gethsemane, at the base of the Mount of Olives. On this mountain, overlooking Jerusalem, Jesus taught His disciples to pray. This is where He wept over the city. This is where He will plant His feet when He comes back in glory, not far from where the cross was plunged into Mount Calvary. This is called Victory!

Then His kingdom will branch out—just as the crown of a tree, by its branches, covers a great area. The Branch protects and hovers over His own, and "His beauty shall be like an olive tree" (Hosea 14:6).

THE ROOT, THE BRANCH, THE VINE

Years ago, I preached a sermon titled "The Cradle, the Cross, and the Crown"—all made from God's creation–the tree. But there is no greater sermon than what is found in Isaiah when He prophesied the tremendous life of the Lord Jesus Christ.

Isaiah wrote:

> For He shall grow up . . . as a tender plant,
> And as a root out of dry ground. . . .
> He was wounded for our transgressions. (53:2–5)

And He died with a crown of thorns piercing His brow. The Babe would be named Immanuel, God with us. (Isa. 7:14)

Jesus was born among His very creation, and it isn't

hard to imagine the animals bowing in reverence as they welcomed the Child—who would be King—into the world.

Job wrote:

> There is hope for a tree,
> If it is cut down, that it will sprout again,
> And that its tender shoots will not cease. (14:7)

The world thought they had conquered the King of the Jews when they crucified Him on the cross, but Peter wrote that while Jesus bore our sins in His own body "on the tree" (1 Pet. 2:24), the seed would live again—and He did. No wonder the Branch is coming back to reign (Isa. 9:7).

This is eternity—it is coming. Revelation is a book that thrills the heart. It is a book of action because its message calls out to mankind with repetition: Behold! Come!

Why? There is something magnificent to behold that is yet to come!

The apostle John is told, "[Come up here—come and see!] Behold, the Lion of the tribe of Judah, the Root of David" (Rev. 5:5). Then we're told that Heaven will come down; hold fast till the Lord comes. The nations will gather and come to worship Him. No wonder the Spirit tells us to come; let him who thirsts come drink, and the Lord proclaims, "Behold, I make all things new" (21:5).

Behold! "The marriage of the Lamb has come" (19:7).

Come! "Gather together for the supper of the great God" (v. 17).

Where does the King want us to come? Home.

This little word *come* is filled with eternal promise. I suppose that is why I have always been drawn to the song that closed most of our evangelistic crusades:

And as thou bidst me come to Thee,

O Lamb of God, I come, I come.[1]

Jesus gives us His words:

"*I am* the Alpha and the Omega, the Beginning and the End . . . who is and who was and who is to come." (Rev. 1:8)

"I, Jesus, have sent My angel to testify to you these things. . . . *I am* the Root and the Offspring of David, the Bright and Morning Star." (22:16)

He who testifies to these things says, "Surely I am coming quickly." (v. 20)

He sends out a mighty promise: "He who overcomes . . . I will write on him My new name" (3:12).

The Bible says, "He is Lord of lords and King of kings; and those who are with Him are called, chosen, and faithful"

(17:14). The chosen are those who have received Him as personal Savior. When we are with Him for eternity, we will inherit a new address—Heaven—and it is all the address we'll need. We will also inherit our new names. And we will eat the fruit from the Vine of the tree that possesses eternal life in Christ Jesus our Lord.

No wonder He came—that we might come.

The great revelation for me is to know that when the Lord calls me home, *where I am* then, is where He will be, waiting in the place He has prepared from the beginning. This is the Eternal Reign of the Great I Am.

No wonder He is the Prince of Peace.

No wonder He is King!

[God] has delivered us from the power of darkness and conveyed us into the kingdom of the Son of His love, in whom we have redemption . . . having made peace through the blood of His cross. (Col. 1:13–14, 20)

CHAPTER 7

LIVING LIFE
WITH HOPE

Because Jesus conquered death
on the cross, we have a living hope
through the resurrection of Christ.

A Cornell University Medical College professor once said, "Hope, like faith, is medicinal." Hope is both biologically and psychologically vital to the human race.

It has always been a great privilege for me to speak to students on college and university campuses. Young people by nature are truth seekers, but many often get bogged down by theoretical ideals that hinder truth. They graduate with more knowledge than ever before, but walk into a hopeless future with more questions left unanswered.

I can recall being approached by a sophomore who asked, "Mr. Graham, you won't let us down, will you?" Puzzled, I asked him what he meant. He explained, "Please tell us how to find God."

On another campus a student said, "Mr. Graham, we hear a lot about what Christ has done for us, the value of religion, and what personal salvation is. But nobody tells us how to find Christ."

This lament of an honest student became a challenge to me to explain simply and plainly how to find Christ. This is the critical and clear message of Scripture, and it is my desire to proclaim its life-changing truth.

God has made the plan of redemption plain. Finding Jesus Christ and having the assurance of His salvation is essential to securing eternal life with Him in Heaven.

But even when a preacher makes the message plain, it is God's Spirit that opens a person's understanding. I had the privilege of preaching the Gospel on every continent in most of the countries of the world, and I have found that when I present the simple message of the Gospel of Jesus Christ, with authority, quoting from the very Word of God—He takes that message and drives it supernaturally into the human heart.

I remember a young reporter in Glasgow who attended our meetings at Kelvin Hall as part of his assignment. He heard the Gospel night after night, but it seemed to make no impact upon him.

One day, however, a colleague asked him, "What are they preaching down there?" He tried to explain the Gospel he had heard, and in so doing, he found himself saying, "You see, it's this way. Christ died for me. . . . Christ died for my sins." And when he said that, he suddenly realized the words were true! The full meaning of the message burst in miraculously upon him, and then and there he received salvation by acknowledging his sin, receiving Christ's work on the cross for the forgiveness of his sin, committing himself wholly to Jesus Christ, and having the assurance of life everlasting. I have never known anyone to receive the Lord and ever regret it. What about you? If you don't know Him yet, ask Jesus to open your heart to Him.

RECOGNIZING YOUR SPIRITUAL NEED

You must be convinced that you need God's salvation. If you feel that you are self-sufficient, capable of meeting life head-on and under your own power, then you will never find Him. A reading of the Gospels will reveal that Jesus did not impose Himself upon those who felt self-sufficient, righteous, and self-confident.

There must be recognition of your own sinfulness and spiritual need before there can be a response from Christ. He came to call not the righteous but sinners to repentance. Many divine promises hinge on a condition: "*If* we walk in the light . . . the blood of Jesus Christ His Son cleanses us from all sin. . . . *If* we confess our sins, He is faithful and just to forgive us our sins and to cleanse us from all unrighteousness" (1 John 1:7, 9).

UNDERSTANDING THE
MESSAGE OF THE CROSS

You must understand that the message Jesus proclaimed from the cross was to come to Him with all your sin, and repent. Many great theologians have never understood the lessons of the cross. Many intellectuals have made up theories as to why Christ died and the eternal significance of His death. None of the theories seem to satisfy.

The Bible says that the natural man cannot comprehend the things of God, so how can people understand what happened at the cross? It is only when we understand that Christ died in the place of sinners, for sin, that we find the elements of forgiveness. Jesus was born with the cross darkening His pathway. From the cradle to the cross, Jesus' purpose was to die so that mankind may live.

Here is where the miracle lies. Just as the apostle Peter by a divine revelation said, "You are the Christ, the Son of the living God" (Matt. 16:16), so by a miracle the meaning of the cross will be given to you by the Holy Spirit of God.

COUNTING THE COST

You must count the cost. This is what I explained to one of the students seeking truth. It is important to note that Jesus discouraged superficial enthusiasm. He urged people to consider the cost of being His disciple: "If anyone desires to come after Me, let him deny himself, and take up his cross daily, and follow Me" (Luke 9:23). Jesus said, "Count the cost . . . whoever of you does not forsake all that he has cannot be My disciple" (Luke 14:28, 33).

Part of counting the cost is realizing that when this transformation takes place, you will become a target of Satan, who is the enemy of Christ. When you walk Satan's way in the world, he doesn't go out of his way to bother you. He has you; you are his child. But when you become a Christian, a child of God, Satan will use all of his diabolical techniques to thwart, hinder, and defeat you. Have you considered the cost?

ACKNOWLEDGING HIM AS SAVIOR AND LORD

You must confess and acknowledge Jesus Christ as Lord of your life. I have always asked people to make this public confession in our meetings because Jesus in His earthly ministry demanded a definite commitment. He had reasons for demanding that people openly follow Him. Jesus knew that an unwitnessed vow is no vow at all. Until you have surrendered to Christ by a conscious act of your will, you are not a Christian.

BREAKING SIN'S BONDAGE

You must believe what the Bible says: We are all sinners; we have broken God's law and His commandments. We have turned our backs on Him. That is a very dangerous thing for our country, for us as individuals, and for our families. People don't want to believe they are sinners. Sin is a disease of the human heart. It affects the mind, and the will, and the emotion; every part of our being. This is why the cross offends; it directly confronts the evil that dominates so much of the world. We deserve Hell; we deserve judgment and all that it means.

How can we break this bondage? How can we be set free? God helps us break these chains. I want to tell people about the meaning of the cross—not a cross that hangs around our necks. The cross is where Jesus Christ took upon Himself the sins of the world. God can make us totally new. God's Word demands—it doesn't suggest—it demands a new life in Christ—and He will help us overcome sin.

The Bible says, "Therefore, if anyone is in Christ, he is a new creation; old things have passed away; behold, all things have become new" (2 Cor. 5:17).

TAKING YOUR FIRST STEP

You must be willing to take a definite step in obedience to Jesus. Jesus stepped out of Glory and picked up His cross for you. Will you obey and follow Him? The Bible says, "As many as received Him, to them He gave the right to become children of God, to those who believe in His name" (John 1:12). You must be willing for God to change your life.

When you come to Christ, you are considered a spiritual

baby. As you read the New Testament, you will see how the early disciples, during the first days of following Christ, faltered and often failed. They quarreled, they were envious, they were contentious, they were unfaithful, and they often grew angry.

However, as they became emptied of self and filled with Christ, they developed into the fullness of the stature of a Christian. This is what Christ empowers you to do as you walk in new life with Him.

HAVING ASSURANCE OF KNOWING CHRIST

You must receive the faith God empowers. How vivid, how alive, the cross becomes when the apostle Paul speaks of it: "I have been crucified with Christ; it is no longer I who live, but Christ lives in me" (Gal. 2:20). When you see Him high and lifted up—the Son of God smitten, marred, bruised, and dying for you—and understand that He loves you and gave Himself for you, you will have taken a step toward the Christian's assurance of salvation.

Many struggle because they want Christ to walk with

them, but believers are instructed to leave their own pathways and walk with Christ. He comes in and saves us, and then we place ourselves completely in Him. Conversion is the first step to this wonderful new journey. A new life begins the moment you receive Christ and the Holy Spirit takes up residence. During the rest of your lifetime, God will be busy conforming you to the image of His Son, the Lord Jesus Christ. This is how we prepare to meet our God.

And this is "the mystery which has been hidden from ages and from generations, but now has been revealed to His saints. To them God willed to make known what are the riches of the glory of this mystery . . . which is Christ in you, the hope of glory . . . which works in me mightily" (Col. 1:26–27, 29).

DESIRING GOD'S WORD

You will desire nourishment from God's Word when you accept Jesus as your Savior, by faith. Be faithful in reading the Bible, praying for God's guidance and strength each day, seeking the fellowship of other believers as part of Christ's church, and sharing your new faith with those who are still wandering in darkness. The church is the Body of Christ on earth, and it is important to join with other followers of Jesus Christ to learn from one another and to encourage one another.

I cannot imagine living in a world without other believers. In all of my travels around the world, there was always something powerful that happened when I knew I was in the presence of other believers. The Bible calls it a sweet fellowship of the saints. God strengthens us to live for Him (Deut. 33:3; Psa. 50:5; 145:9–10; Acts 2:41–42; and 2 Cor. 8:4).

As you persist in Bible study, prayer, and fellowship in the church, you'll find yourself growing. Christ will work in you and through you, and you will be able to say with Paul, "I can do all things through Christ who strengthens me" (Phil. 4:13). You will find miracles happening all around you as you discipline your life to the pattern of a true Christian.

JESUS IS CALLING-YOU

Would you like to know that every sin is forgiven? Would you like to know that you are ready to meet God? You can live life with this hope today, if you will let Christ transform your heart.

The Bible says that "whoever calls on the name of the LORD shall be saved" (Rom. 10:13).

He extends an invitation to you. Will you open the door to Him right now? You can do so by praying honestly and sincerely,

O God, I am a sinner. I repent of my sin. Forgive me and help me turn from my sin. I acknowledge what You have done on the cross for me and receive Your Son, Jesus Christ, as my Savior. I confess Him as my Lord. Give me faith to believe and trust as You lead me into obedience, relying on You in all things. Thank You for redeeming me and making me Your disciple. In Jesus' name. Amen.

No transcribed prayer grants a sinner salvation, but the Bible is clear that we must recognize our sin and repent of it, be willing for God to change us, and obediently follow Jesus Christ.

This is the most important step anyone can take in life and is the only way to truth. If you have entered into this new life, pray and ask the Lord to direct you to a Bible-believing, Bible-preaching church, where you can grow in the truth of God's Word and fellowship with His people.

Then please write to the following address so

information can be sent to help you in your new journey with the resurrected Christ. God bless you.

Write to:

Billy Graham Evangelistic Association

1 Billy Graham Parkway

Charlotte, NC 28201-0001

www.bgea.org

1-877-2GRAHAM (1-877-247-2426)

For more information on The Billy Graham Library: billygrahamlibrary.org

And the Lord added

to the church daily

those who were being

saved (Acts 2:47).

AFTERWORD

On the morning of February 21, 2018, my grandfather, Billy Graham, slipped silently and sweetly into the presence of Jesus. He was called home in a manner that was fitting for a servant of Christ who had uncompromisingly proclaimed "the Way, the Truth, and the Life" for the better part of a century.

He closed his eyes in the earthly realm, only to open them once again in Heaven.

I believe it was something that my grandfather anticipated with great joy and peace. Why? Because he knew—with no doubt in his mind—that it wasn't the end. Death for him was just a door that must be walked through in order to get to his real and true home.

"One day you're going to hear that Billy Graham has died," he once said, somber and serious, yet filled with hope and peace. "But don't believe it! For on that day I will be more alive than ever before. I will have just changed addresses!"

Such faith and surety could only be found in the cross. It had nothing to do with my grandfather's lifetime of service and ministry, all the good things he did and the people he helped. Rather, it had everything to do with Jesus' death and resurrection, His sacrifice and victory.

When I think of my grandfather, that image of the cross comes to mind. His life, his ministry, his calling— everything he was and had revolved around the cross of Jesus Christ. It was the hope to which he clung, the promise of eternity he proclaimed.

It makes me smile to think of my grandfather's preaching. He would start with a variety of Bible verses and anecdotes, but he would quickly pivot and race directly to the cross. He did it every time because the cross is the source of our salvation. The words of Billy Graham had no power to change anybody, but Christ's finished work on the cross—the wages of our sin paid in full—altered the course of eternity.

When he'd reach the end of his message, he would invite people to respond to the cross, surrendering their life and eternity to their Savior. It wasn't a soft plea, but a supernaturally bold declaration: "Come now! We'll wait on you. You come!"

Thousands would pour forward, soft hearts open to the loving grace of Jesus. Throughout the years I had the opportunity to sit on stage with my grandfather, and tears would fill my eyes as I saw the multitude who were dead in their sins, made alive together with Christ (Eph. 2:5).

It has now been years since my grandfather's passing, and I still miss him dearly. The world knew Billy Graham, but I knew him as Daddy Bill. The world knew an incredible orator, but I knew the man who liked to sit quietly and listen to others. The world knew a giant of the faith, but I knew the man who would kneel to envelop his grandson in a big embrace.

Because of the cross, I know that I will see my grandfather again. Since Christ has conquered death, it is now subservient to Him. Death has lost its sting (1 Cor. 15:55). For those who call on the name of Jesus as Savior and Lord— like my grandfather—death is now the friend that opens the door and introduces us to eternity with Jesus in Heaven.

If you have not yet done that, it's not too late. Take your opportunity now to follow in my grandfather's footsteps by clinging to the cross, surrendering your eternity to the One who paid the price for your sin. Jesus is waiting with open arms to welcome you home.

Will Graham

PRAYING THE SCRIPTURES

(NKJV translation)

GOD'S LOVE

For God so loved the world that he gave his one
and only Son, that whoever believes in him shall
not perish but have eternal life. **John 3:16**

But God demonstrates His own love toward
us, in that while we were still sinners,
Christ died for us. **Romans 5:8**

Behold what manner of love the Father
has bestowed on us, that we should
be called children of God! Therefore
the world does not know us, because
it did not know Him. **1 John 3:1**

And we have known and believed the love that God
has for us. God is love, and he who abides in love
abides in God, and God in him. **1 John 4:16**

I have been crucified with Christ; it is no longer I who live, but Christ lives in me; and the *life* which I now live in the flesh I live by faith in the Son of God, who loved me and gave Himself for me. **Galatians 2:20**

We love Him because He first loved us. **1 John 4:19**

Beloved, let us love one another, for love is of God; and everyone who loves is born of God and knows God. He who does not love does not know God, for God is love. **1 John 4:7–8**

But God, who is rich in mercy, because of His great love with which He loved us, even when we were dead in trespasses, made us alive together with Christ (by grace you have been saved). **Ephesians 2:4–5**

The Lord has appeared of old to me, *saying*: "Yes, I have loved you with an everlasting love; Therefore with lovingkindness I have drawn you. **Jeremiah 31:3**

Therefore know that the Lord your God, He *is* God, the
faithful God who keeps covenant and mercy for a
thousand generations with those who love Him and
keep His commandments. **Deuteronomy 7:9**

How precious *is* Your lovingkindness, O God!
Therefore the children of men put their trust
under the shadow of Your wings. **Psalm 36:7**

This is My commandment, that you love one
another as I have loved you. **John 15:12**

SALVATION

For by grace you have been saved through faith,
and that not of yourselves; *it is* the gift of God, not
of works, lest anyone should boast. **Ephesians 2:8–9**

Not by works of righteousness which we have
done, but according to His mercy He saved

us, through the washing of regeneration and renewing of the Holy Spirit. **Titus 3:5**

That if you confess with your mouth the Lord Jesus and believe in your heart that God has raised Him from the dead, you will be saved. For with the heart one believes unto righteousness, and with the mouth confession is made unto salvation. **Romans 10:9–10**

Nor is there salvation in any other, for there is no other name under heaven given among men by which we must be saved. **Acts 4:12**

Jesus said to him, "I am the way, the truth, and the life. No one comes to the Father except through Me." **John 14:6**

No one can come to Me unless the Father who sent Me draws him; and I will raise him up at the last day. **John 6:44**

But the salvation of the righteous is from the Lord; *He is* their strength in the time of trouble. **Psalm 37:39**

Salvation *belongs* to the Lord. Your blessing *is* upon Your people. *Selah* **Psalm 3:8**

Then Peter said to them, "Repent, and let every one of you be baptized in the name of Jesus Christ for the remission of sins; and you shall receive the gift of the Holy Spirit." **Acts 2:38**

For God did not send His Son into the world to condemn the world, but that the world through Him might be saved. **John 3:17**

"He who believes in Him is not condemned; but he who does not believe is condemned already, because he has not believed in the name of the only begotten Son of God. And this is the condemnation, that the light has come into the world, and men loved darkness rather than light, because their deeds were evil. For everyone practicing evil hates the light and does not come to the light, lest his deeds should be exposed. But he who does the truth comes to the light, that his deeds may be clearly seen, that they have been done in God." **John 3:17–21**

For the wages of sin *is* death, but the gift of God *is* eternal life in Christ Jesus our Lord. **Romans 6:23**

And they came to John and said to him, "Rabbi, He who was with you beyond the Jordan, to whom you have testified—behold, He is baptizing, and all are coming to Him!" **John 3:26**

FORGIVENESS

And be kind to one another, tenderhearted, forgiving one another, even as God in Christ forgave you. **Ephesians 4:32**

And whenever you stand praying, if you have anything against anyone, forgive him, that your Father in heaven may also forgive you your trespasses. **Mark 11:25**

If we confess our sins, He is faithful and just to forgive us *our* sins and to cleanse us from all unrighteousness. **1 John 1:9**

For if you forgive men their trespasses, your heavenly Father will also forgive you. But if you do not forgive men their trespasses, neither will your Father forgive your trespasses. **Matthew 6:14–15**

Bearing with one another, and forgiving one another, if anyone has a complaint against another; even as Christ forgave you, so you also *must do*. **Colossians 3:13**

Confess *your* trespasses to one another, and pray for one another, that you may be healed. The effective, fervent prayer of a righteous man avails much. **James 5:16**

He has not dealt with us according to our sins, nor punished us according to our iniquities. For as the heavens are high above the earth, *so* great is His mercy toward those who fear Him; as far as the east is from the west, *so* far has He removed our transgressions from us. As a father pities *his* children, *so* the Lord pities those who fear Him. For He knows our frame; He remembers that we *are* dust. **Psalm 103:10–14**

Hatred stirs up strife, but love covers all sins. **Proverbs 10:12**

In Him we have redemption through His blood, the forgiveness of sins, according to the riches of His grace. **Ephesians 1:7**

For all have sinned and fall short of the glory of God. **Romans 3:23**

For this is My blood of the new covenant, which is shed for many for the remission of sins. **Matthew 26:28**

For You, Lord, *are* good, and ready to
forgive, and abundant in mercy to all those
who call upon You. **Psalm 86:5**

PEACE

These things I have spoken to you, that in Me you may
have peace. In the world you will have tribulation; but
be of good cheer, I have overcome the world. **John 16:33**

Now may the Lord of peace Himself give you
peace always in every way. The Lord *be* with
you all. **2 Thessalonians 3:16**

You will keep *him* in perfect peace,
Whose mind *is* stayed *on You*, Because
he trusts in You. **Isaiah 26:3**

Be anxious for nothing, but in everything by
prayer and supplication, with thanksgiving,

let your requests be made known to
God; and the peace of God, which surpasses
all understanding, will guard your hearts and
minds through Christ Jesus. **Philippians 4:6–7**

Peace I leave with you, My peace I give to you; not as
the world gives do I give to you. Let not your heart
be troubled, neither let it be afraid. **John 14:27**

And let the peace of God rule in your
hearts, to which also you were called in one
body; and be thankful. **Colossians 3:15**

Casting all your care upon Him, for
He cares for you. **1 Peter 5:7**

Therefore, having been justified by
faith, we have peace with God through
our Lord Jesus Christ. **Romans 5:1**

Now the fruit of righteousness is sown in peace
by those who make peace. **James 3:18**

For God is not *the author* of confusion but of peace, as
in all the churches of the saints. **1 Corinthians 14:33**

When a man's ways please the Lord, He makes even
his enemies to be at peace with him. **Proverbs 16:7**

Finally, all *of you be* of one mind, having
compassion for one another; love as
brothers, *be* tenderhearted, *be* courteous; not
returning evil for evil or reviling for reviling, but on
the contrary blessing, knowing that you were called
to this, that you may inherit a blessing. For "He who
would love life and see good days, let him refrain
his tongue from evil, and his lips from speaking
deceit. Let him turn away from evil and do good;
let him seek peace and pursue it. **1 Peter 3:8–11**

HOPE

For I know the thoughts that I think toward you,
says the Lord, thoughts of peace and not of evil, to
give you a future and a hope. **Jeremiah 29:11**

Now may the God of hope fill you with all joy and
peace in believing, that you may abound in hope
by the power of the Holy Spirit. **Romans 15:13**

But those who wait on the Lord shall
renew *their* strength; They shall mount up with
wings like eagles, they shall run and not be weary,
they shall walk and not faint. **Isaiah 40:31**

For whatever things were written before were written for
our learning, that we through the patience and comfort
of the Scriptures might have hope. **Romans 15:4**

And now, Lord, what do I wait for?
My hope is in You. **Psalm 39:7**

Now hope does not disappoint, because the love of God has been poured out in our hearts by the Holy Spirit who was given to us. **Romans 5:5**

For surely there is a hereafter, and your hope will not be cut off. **Proverbs 23:18**

Fear not, for I *am* with you; be not dismayed, for I *am* your God. I will strengthen you, Yes, I will help you, I will uphold you with My righteous right hand. **Isaiah 41:10**

This *hope* we have as an anchor of the soul, both sure and steadfast, and which enters the *Presence* behind the veil. **Hebrews 6:19**

You *are* my hiding place and my shield; I hope in Your word. **Psalm 119:114**

Therefore I also, after I heard of your faith
in the Lord Jesus and your love for all the
saints, do not cease to give thanks for you,
making mention of you in my prayers: that the
God of our Lord Jesus Christ, the Father of
glory, may give to you the spirit of wisdom
and revelation in the knowledge of Him, the
eyes of your understanding being enlightened;
that you may know what is the hope of His
calling, what are the riches of the glory of His
inheritance in the saints. **Ephesians 1:15-18**

And everyone who has this hope in Him purifies
himself, just as He is pure. **1 John 3:3**

Therefore gird up the loins of your mind,
be sober, and rest *your* hope fully upon the
grace that is to be brought to you at the
revelation of Jesus Christ. **1 Peter 1:13**

THE CROSS OF CHRIST

Looking unto Jesus, the author and finisher
of *our* faith, who for the joy that was set
before Him endured the cross, despising the
shame, and has sat down at the right hand
of the throne of God. **Hebrews 12:2**

But God forbid that I should boast except in the cross
of our Lord Jesus Christ, by whom the world has been
crucified to me, and I to the world. **Galatians 6:14**

But He *was* wounded for our transgressions,
He was bruised for our iniquities; The
chastisement for our peace *was* upon Him, And
by His stripes we are heated. **Isaiah 53:5**

For the message of the cross is foolishness to those
who are perishing, but to us who are being saved
it is the power of God. **1 Corinthians 1:18**

For to this you were called, because Christ also suffered for us, leaving us an example, that you should follow His steps: "Who committed no sin, nor was deceit found in His mouth"; who, when He was reviled, did not revile in return; when He suffered, He did not threaten, but committed *Himself* to Him who judges righteously; who Himself bore our sins in His own body on the tree, that we, having died to sins, might live for righteousness— by whose stripes you were healed. **Peter 2:21-24**

And he who does not take his cross and follow after Me is not worthy of Me. **Matthew 10:38**

When He had called the people to *Himself,* with His disciples also, He said to them, "Whoever desires to come after Me, let him deny himself, and take up his cross, and follow Me." **Mark 8:34**

For it pleased *the Father that* in Him all the fullness should dwell, and by Him to reconcile all things to Himself, by Him, whether things on earth or things in heaven, having made peace through the blood of His cross. **Colossians 1:19-20**

And you, being dead in your trespasses and the uncircumcision of your flesh, He has made alive together with Him, having forgiven you all trespasses, having wiped out the handwriting of requirements that was against us, which was contrary to us. And He has taken it out of the way, having nailed it to the cross. **Colossians 2:13-14**

For if we have been united together in the likeness of His death, certainly we also shall be *in the likeness of His* resurrection, knowing this, that our old man was crucified with *Him*, that the body of sin might be done away with, that we should no longer be slaves of sin. **Romans 6:5-6**

And being found in appearance as a man, He humbled Himself and became obedient to *the point of* death, even the death of the cross. **Philippians 2:8**

JOURNEY OF FAITH

For we walk by faith, not by sight. **2 Corinthians 5:7**

But without faith *it is* impossible to please *Him*, for
he who comes to God must believe that He
is, and *that* He is a rewarder of those who
diligently seek Him. **Hebrews 11:6**

Now faith is the substance of things hoped for,
the evidence of things not seen. **Hebrews 11:1**

So Jesus answered and said to them, "Have faith in
God. For assuredly, I say to you, whoever says to
this mountain, 'Be removed and be cast into the
sea,' and does not doubt in his heart, but believes
that those things he says will be done, he will have
whatever he says. Therefore I say to you, whatever
things you ask when you pray, believe that you
receive them, and you will have *them.* **Mark 11:22–24**

You see then that a man is justified by works,
and not by faith only. **James 2:24**

So Jesus said to them, "Because of your unbelief;
for assuredly, I say to you, if you have faith as a
mustard seed, you will say to this mountain, 'Move
from here to there,' and it will move; and nothing
will be impossible for you. **Matthew 17:20**

I have fought the good fight, I have finished the
race, I have kept the faith. **2 Timothy 4:7**

For whatever is born of God overcomes
the world. And this is the victory that has
overcome the world—our faith. **1 John 5:4**

Knowing that a man is not justified by the works of the
law but by faith in Jesus Christ, even we have believed
in Christ Jesus, that we might be justified by faith in
Christ and not by the works of the law; for by the works
of the law no flesh shall be justified. **Galatians 2:16**

Stand therefore, having girded your waist with truth, having put on the breastplate of righteousness, and having shod your feet with the preparation of the gospel of peace; above all, taking the shield of faith with which you will be able to quench all the fiery darts of the wicked one. **Ephesians 6:14-16**

For in it the righteousness of God is revealed from faith to faith; as it is written, "The just shall live by faith." **Romans 1:17**

In this you greatly rejoice, though now for a little while, if need be, you have been grieved by various trials, that the genuineness of your faith, *being* much more precious than gold that perishes, though it is tested by fire, may be found to praise, honor, and glory at the revelation of Jesus Christ. **1 Peter 1:6-7**

RESURRECTION

Jesus said to her, "I am the resurrection and
the life. He who believes in Me, though he
may die, he shall live." **John 11:25**

Blessed *be* the God and Father of our Lord Jesus
Christ, who according to His abundant mercy has
begotten us again to a living hope through the
resurrection of Jesus Christ from the dead. **1 Peter 1:3**

But if the Spirit of Him who raised Jesus from the
dead dwells in you, He who raised Christ from the
dead will also give life to your mortal bodies through
His Spirit who dwells in you. **Romans 8:11**

And this is the will of Him who sent Me, that
everyone who sees the Son and believes in
Him may have everlasting life; and I will
raise him up at the last day. **John 6:40**

And God both raised up the Lord and will also raise us up by His power. **1 Corinthians 6:14**

Your dead shall live; *Together with* my dead body they shall arise. Awake and sing, you who dwell in dust; for your dew *is like* the dew of herbs, and the earth shall cast out the dead. **Isaiah 26:19**

And you will be blessed, because they cannot repay you; for you shall be repaid at the resurrection of the just. **Luke 14:14**

Yet indeed I also count all things loss for the excellence of the knowledge of Christ Jesus my Lord, for whom I have suffered the loss of all things, and count them as rubbish, that I may gain Christ and be found in Him, not having my own righteousness, which *is* from the law, but that which *is* through faith in Christ, the righteousness which is from God by faith; that I may know Him and the power of His resurrection, and the fellowship of His sufferings, being conformed to His death. **Philippians 3:8-10**

Now if we died with Christ, we believe that we shall also live with Him, knowing that Christ, having been raised from the dead, dies no more. Death no longer has dominion over Him. For *the death* that He died, He died to sin once for all; but *the life* that He lives, He lives to God. Likewise you also, reckon yourselves to be dead indeed to sin, but alive to God in Christ Jesus our Lord. **Romans 6:8–11**

Do not marvel at this; for the hour is coming in which all who are in the graves will hear His voice and come forth—those who have done good, to the resurrection of life, and those who have done evil, to the resurrection of condemnation. **John 5:28–29**

Then He said to them, "Thus it is written, and thus it was necessary for the Christ to suffer and to rise

from the dead the third day, and that repentance
and remission of sins should be preached in His name to
all nations, beginning at Jerusalem. **Luke 24:46–47**

For since by man *came* death, by Man also *came* the
resurrection of the dead. **1 Corinthians 15:21**

ETERNAL LIFE

For the wages of sin *is* death, but the [a]
gift of God *is* eternal life in Christ
Jesus our Lord. **Romans 6:23**

And this is eternal life, that they may
know You, the only true God, and Jesus
Christ whom You have sent. **John 17:3**

Most assuredly, I say to you, he who hears My word
and believes in Him who sent Me has everlasting

life, and shall not come into judgment, but
has passed from death into life. **John 5:24**

He who believes in the Son has everlasting life; and
he who does not believe the Son shall not see life,
but the wrath of God abides on him. **John 3:36**

Do not be deceived, God is not mocked;
for whatever a man sows, that he will also reap. For
he who sows to his flesh will of the flesh reap
corruption, but he who sows to the Spirit will of
the Spirit reap everlasting life. **Galatians 6:7–8**

For I am persuaded that neither death nor life,
nor angels nor principalities nor powers, nor
things present nor things to come, nor height
nor depth, nor any other created thing, shall be
able to separate us from the love of God which
is in Christ Jesus our Lord. **Romans 8:38–39**

And this is the promise that He has
promised us—eternal life. **1 John 2:25**

However, for this reason I obtained mercy, that in
me first Jesus Christ might show all longsuffering,
as a pattern to those who are going to believe
on Him for everlasting life. **1 Timothy 1:16**

These things I have written to you who believe in
the name of the Son of God, that you may know
that you have eternal life, and that you may *continue*
to believe in the name of the Son of God. **1 John 5:13**

Most assuredly, I say to you, he who believes
in Me has everlasting life. **John 6:47**

My sheep hear My voice, and I know them, and
they follow Me. And I give them eternal life,
and they shall never perish; neither shall anyone
snatch them out of My hand. **John 10:27–28**

And this is the testimony: that God has given us eternal life, and this life is in His Son. **1 John 5:11**

CLEANSING BLOOD OF CHRIST

How much more shall the blood of Christ, who through the eternal Spirit offered Himself without spot to God, cleanse your conscience from dead works to serve the living God? **Hebrews 9:14**

But if we walk in the light as He is in the light, we have fellowship with one another, and the blood of Jesus Christ His Son cleanses us from all sin. **1 John 1:7**

For the life of the flesh *is* in the blood, and I have given it to you upon the altar to make atonement for your souls; for it *is* the blood *that* makes atonement for the soul. **Leviticus 17:11**

Much more then, having now been
justified by His blood, we shall be saved from
wrath through Him. **Romans 5:9**

Therefore take heed to yourselves and to all the
flock, among which the Holy Spirit has made you
overseers, to shepherd the church of God which
He purchased with His own blood. **Acts 20:28**

Not with the blood of goats and calves, but with His
own blood He entered the Most Holy Place once for
all, having obtained eternal redemption. **Hebrews 9:12**

In the same manner *He* also *took* the cup after
supper, saying, "This cup is the new covenant in
My blood. This do, as often as you drink *it,* in
remembrance of Me." **1 Corinthians 11:25**

But now in Christ Jesus you who once
were far off have been brought near by
the blood of Christ. **Ephesians 2:13**

And according to the law almost all things are purified with blood, and without shedding of blood there is no remission. **Hebrews 9:22**

And I said to him, [a]"Sir, you know." So he said to me, "These are the ones who come out of the great tribulation, and washed their robes and made them white in the blood of the Lamb. **Revelation 7:14**

Knowing that you were not redeemed with [a] corruptible things, *like* silver or gold, from your aimless conduct *received* by tradition from your fathers, but with the precious blood of Christ, as of a lamb without blemish and without spot. **1 Peter 1:18–19**

And when He had given thanks, He broke *it* and said, "Take, eat; this is My body which is broken for you; do this in remembrance of Me." In the same manner *He* also *took* the cup after supper, saying, "This cup is the new covenant in My blood. This do, as often as you drink *it,* in remembrance of Me." For as often as

you eat this bread and drink this cup, you proclaim the
Lord's death till He comes.**1 Corinthians 11:24–26**

REDEMPTION

He has delivered us from the power of
darkness and conveyed *us* into the kingdom of the Son
of His love, in whom we have redemption through His
blood, the forgiveness of sins. **Colossians 1:13–14**

He has sent redemption to His people; He
has commanded His covenant forever: Holy
and awesome *is* His name. **Psalm 111:9**

But of Him you are in Christ Jesus, who became
for us wisdom from God—and righteousness and
sanctification and redemption. **1 Corinthians 1:30**

For all have sinned and fall short of the glory of
God, being justified freely by His grace through

the redemption that is in Christ Jesus, whom
God set forth *as* a propitiation by His blood,
through faith, to demonstrate His righteousness,
because in His forbearance God had passed
over the sins that were previously committed, to
demonstrate at the present time His righteousness,
that He might be just and the justifier of the one
who has faith in Jesus. **Romans 3:23–26**

Let the redeemed of the Lord say *so*, whom He has
redeemed from the hand of the enemy. **Psalm 107:2**

I have blotted out, like a thick cloud, your
transgressions, and like a cloud, your sins. Return
to Me, for I have redeemed you. **Isaiah 44:22**

Christ has redeemed us from the curse
of the law, having become a curse for us
(for it is written, "Cursed *is* everyone who
hangs on a tree") **Galatians 3:13**

And for this reason He is the Mediator of the new covenant, by means of death, for the redemption of the transgressions under the first covenant, that those who are called may receive the promise of the eternal inheritance. **Hebrews 9:15**

Just as the Son of Man did not come to be served, but to serve, and to give his life as a ransom for many. **Matthew 20:28**

But now, thus says the Lord, who created you, O Jacob, and He who formed you, O Israel: "Fear not, for I have redeemed you; I have called *you* by your name; You *are* Mine. When you pass through the waters, I *will be* with you; and through the rivers, they shall not overflow you. When you walk through the fire, you shall not be burned, nor shall the flame scorch you. **Isaiah 43:1–2**

For I know *that* my Redeemer lives, and He shall stand at last on the earth. **Job 19:25**

JESUS THE VICTOR

You are of God, little children, and have overcome
them, because He who is in you is greater
than he who is in the world. **1 John 4:4**

Now thanks *be* to God who always leads us in triumph
in Christ, and through us diffuses the fragrance of
His knowledge in every place. **2 Corinthians 2:14**

But thanks *be* to God, who gives us the victory
through our Lord Jesus Christ. **1 Corinthians 15:57**

For *there is* one God and one Mediator between God
and men, *the* Man Christ Jesus. **1 Timothy 2:5**

I can do all things through Christ who
strengthens me. **Philippians 4:13**

Therefore, if anyone *is* in Christ, *he is* a new creation; old things have passed away; behold, all things have become new. **2 Corinthians 5:17**

Yet in all these things we are more than conquerors through Him who loved us. **Romans 8:37**

For an angel went down at a certain time into the pool and stirred up the water; then whoever stepped in first, after the stirring of the water, was made well of whatever disease he had. **John 5:4**

For sin shall not have dominion over you, for you are not under law but under grace. **Romans 6:14**

The thief does not come except to steal, and to kill, and to destroy. I have come that they may have life, and that they may have *it* more abundantly. **John 10:10**

What then shall we say to these things? If God *is* for us, who *can be* against us? **Romans 8:31**

There is therefore now no condemnation to those who are in Christ Jesus, who do not walk according to the flesh, but according to the Spirit. For the law of the Spirit of life in Christ Jesus has made me free from the law of sin and death. **Romans 8: 1–2**

JESUS AS WORD OF GOD

"Jesus said to them, "Most assuredly, I say to you, before Abraham was, I AM." **John 8:58**

And the Word became flesh and dwelt among us, and we beheld His glory, the glory as of the only begotten of the Father, full of grace and truth. **John 1:14**

I and *My* Father are one. **John 10:30**

For the word of God *is* living and powerful,
and sharper than any two-edged sword, piercing
even to the division of soul and spirit, and of joints
and marrow, and is a discerner of the thoughts
and intents of the heart. **Hebrews 4:12**

So then faith *comes* by hearing, and hearing
by the word of God. **Romans 10:17**

God, who at various times and in various ways spoke
in time past to the fathers by the prophets, has in
these last days spoken to us by *His* Son, whom He has
appointed heir of all things, through whom also He
made the worlds; who being the brightness of *His* glory
and the express image of His person, and upholding
all things by the word of His power, when He had by
Himself purged our sins, sat down at the right hand
of the Majesty on high having become so much better
than the angels, as He has by inheritance obtained
a more excellent name than they. **Hebrews 1:1–4**

He is the image of the invisible God, the firstborn over all creation. **Colossians 1:15**

Yet for us *there is* one God, the Father, of whom *are* all things, and we for Him; and one Lord Jesus Christ, through whom *are* all things, and through whom we *live*. **1 Corinthians 8:6**

Therefore I said to you that you will die in your sins; for if you do not believe that I am *He*, you will die in your sins. **John 8:24**

And Jesus came and spoke to them, saying, "All authority has been given to Me in heaven and on earth." **Matthew 28:18**

And without controversy great is the mystery of godliness: God was manifested in the flesh, justified in the Spirit, seen by angels, preached among the Gentiles, believed on in the world, received up in glory. **1 Timothy 3:16**

TURNING FROM SIN

The Lord is not slack concerning *His* promise, as some count slackness, but is longsuffering toward us, not willing that any should perish but that all should come to repentance. **2 Peter 3:9**

For godly sorrow produces repentance *leading* to salvation, not to be regretted; but the sorrow of the world produces death. **2 Corinthians 7:10**

Repent therefore and be converted, that your sins may be blotted out, so that times of refreshing may come from the presence of the Lord. **Acts 3:19**

Or do you despise the riches of His goodness, forbearance, and longsuffering, not

knowing that the goodness of God leads
you to repentance? **Romans 2:4**

I say to you that likewise there will be more joy in
heaven over one sinner who repents than over ninety-
nine just persons who need no repentance. **Luke 15:7**

I have not come to call *the* righteous, but
sinners, to repentance. **Luke 5:32**

"Therefore I will judge you, O house of Israel, every
one according to his ways," says the Lord God. "Repent,
and turn from all your transgressions, so that
iniquity will not be your ruin." **Ezekiel 18:30**

Whoever has been born of God does not sin,
for His seed remains in him; and he cannot sin,
because he has been born of God. **1 John 3:9**

Jesus answered and said to him, "Most assuredly,
I say to you, unless one is born again, he
cannot see the kingdom of God." **John 3:3**

Likewise, I say to you, there is joy in the presence of the
angels of God over one sinner who repents. **Luke 15:10**

We know that whoever is born of God does not sin;
but he who has been born of God keeps himself, and
the wicked one does not touch him. **1 John 5:18**

For it is God who works in you both to will and
to do for *His* good pleasure. **Philippians 2:13**

WHY JESUS SUFFERED

For I consider that the sufferings of this present
time are not worthy *to be compared* with the glory
which shall be revealed in us. **Romans 8:18**

But rejoice to the extent that you partake of Christ's sufferings, that when His glory is revealed, you may also be glad with exceeding joy. **1 Peter 4:13**

And not only *that,* but we also glory in tribulations, knowing that tribulation produces perseverance; and perseverance, character; and character, hope. Now hope does not disappoint, because the love of God has been poured out in our hearts by the Holy Spirit who was given to us. **Romans 5:3–5**

And God will wipe away every tear from their eyes; there shall be no more death, nor sorrow, nor crying. There shall be no more pain, for the former things have passed away. **Revelation 21:4**

For we do not have a High Priest who cannot sympathize with our weaknesses, but was in all *points* tempted as *we are, yet* without sin. **Hebrews 4:15**

For in that He Himself has suffered, being [a]tempted, He is able to aid those who are tempted. **Hebrews 2:18**

For He made Him who knew no sin *to be* sin for us, that we might become the righteousness of God in Him. **2 Corinthians 5:21**

Blessed *be* the God and Father of our Lord Jesus Christ, the Father of mercies and God of all comfort, who comforts us in all our tribulation, that we may be able to comfort those who are in any trouble, with the comfort with which we ourselves are comforted by God. **2 Corinthians 1:3–4**

The Spirit Himself bears witness with our spirit that we are children of God, and if children, then heirs—heirs of God and joint heirs with Christ, if indeed we suffer with *Him,* that we may also be glorified together. **Romans 8:16-17**

Remember the word that I said to you, 'A servant is not greater than his master.' If they persecuted Me, they will also persecute you. If they kept My word, they will keep yours also. **John 15:20**

NOTES

CHAPTER 1

1. Illustration taken from conversation between Kristy Villa and Donna Lee Toney, during taping of segment on the Billy Graham Library, September 16, 2011, Lifetime TV, *Balancing Act*, cohost Kristy Villa (stage name) for Olga Villaverde, aired October 21, 2011. Used with permission.
2. "The Virgin Birth of Jesus: Fact of Fable?" Religious Tolerance: Ontario Consultants on Religious Tolerance, www.religioustolerance.org/virgin_b.htm.
3. "Do Atheists Deny the Existence or Jesus, or His Resurrection?" comments by Eric_PK and Dave Hitt, Ask the Atheists, May 7–10, 2009, www.asktheatheists.com/questions/433-do-atheists-deny-the-existence-of-Jesus.
4. "Why Are Atheists More Skeptical About Jesus than They Are About Alexander the Great?" question posted on Ask the Atheists, October 25, 2007, www.asktheatheists.com/questions/114-why-are-atheists-more-skeptical-about-jesus.
5. Michael J. Cummings, "The Man of the Millennium," Cummings Study Guides, 2003, www.cummingsstudyguides.net/xbiography.html.

6. Ibid.

7. Derek Jacobi, quoted in Cummings, "Man of the Millennium."

8. Cummings, "Man of the Millennium."

9. "Shakespeare Facts: Read Facts About William Shakespeare," No Sweat Shakespeare, www.nosweatshakespeare.com /resources/shakespeare-facts.

10. Ben Jonson, "Preface to the First Folio (1623)," Shakespeare Online, http://www.shakespeare-online.com/biography /firstfolio.html, italics added.

11. Tom Reedy and David Kathman, "How We Know That Shakespeare Wrote Shakespeare: The Historical Facts," The Shakespeare Authorship Page, http://shakespeareauthorship .com/howdowe.html.

12. Ibid.

13. Cummings, "Man of the Millennium."

14. Ibid.

15. "Shakespeare Facts."

16. John Ankerberg and John Weldon, "The Evidence for the Resurrection of Jesus Christ" (PDF article), 5, Philosophy and Religion, www.philosophy-religion.org/faith/pdfs/resurrection .pdf.

17. *London Law Journal*, 1874, quoted in Irwin H. Linton, *A Lawyer Examines the Bible: A Defense of the Christian Faith* (San Diego: Creation Life Publishers, 1977), 36.

18. Ankerberg and Weldon, "Evidence for the Resurrection of Jesus," 6.

19. *Testimony of the Evangelists by Simon Greenleaf (1783–1853)*, http://law2.umkc.edu/faculty/projects/ftrials/jesus/greenleaf /html, Douglas O. Linder, "The Trial of Jesus: Online Texts

& Links," Famous Trials, umkc School of Law, University of Missouri-Kansas City.

20. William Lyon Phelps, *Human Nature and the Gospel* (1925), quoted in Howard A. Peth, *7 Mysteries Solved: 7 Issues That Touch the Heart of Mankind* (Fallbrook, CA: Hart Research Center), 206.

21. Charles Wesley, "Hymn for Easter Day" (1739), quoted in Collin Hansen, "Hymn for Easter Day," Christian History, http://www.christianitytoday.com/ch/news/2005/mar24.html.

22. Quoted in Ken Ham, "The Bible—'It's Not Historical,'" posted in AnswersinGenesis.org, April 1, 2003, www.answersingenesis .org/articles/au/bible-not-historical.

23. Josephus, *Jewish Antiquities*, 18.3.3, quoted in Gerald Sigal, "Did Flavius Josephus Provide Corroborative Evidence for Christian Claims?" Jews for Judaism, http://www .jewsforjudaism.org/index.php?option=com_content&view =article&id=158:did-flavius-josephus-provides-corroborative -evidence-for-christian-claims&catid=49:trinity&Itemid=501.

24. Tertullian, *Apology*, 5, quoted in Charles Germany, "The Historic Jesus," Rain of God, www.rainofgod.com/Article1.html, September 15, 2008, from T. D. Barnes, *Tertullian: A literary and historical study* (Oxford: 1971).

25. W. O. Clough, ed., *Gesta Pilati; or the Reports, Letters and Acts of Pontius Pilate, Procurator of Judea, with an Account of His Life and Death: Being a Translation and Compilation of All the Writings Ascribed to Him as Made to Tiberius Caesar, Emperor of Rome, Concerning the Life of Jesus, His Trial and Crucifixion* (Indianapolis: Robert Douglass, 1880), http://books.google.com /books?id=IxY3AAAAMAAJ&pg=PA1&source=gbs_selected _pages&cad=3#v=onepage&q&f=false.

26. Julian the Apostate, quoted in Charles Germany, "The Historic Jesus," Rain of God, www.rainofgod.com/Article1.html, September 15, 2008, from *Against the Galileans*, (1923), 313–17.

27. Charles Germany, "The Historic Jesus," Rain of God, www.rainofgod.com/Article1.html, September 15, 2008. The phrase, "Vicisti, Galilaee," introduces Algernon Charles Swinburne's "Hymn to Proserpine" (1866), in which the poet imagines what Julian might have felt about the rise of Christianity. This poem may be found on The Victorian Web, http://www.victorianweb.org/authors/swinburne/hymn.html.

28. Plato, *Five Great Dialogues*, ed. and introduced by Louise Ropes Loomis, tr. B. Jowett (Princeton, NJ: Van Nostrand, 1942), 37, 38, 47. "I know that I know nothing," is the present-day recollection of the famous quote.

29. Louis Ropes Loomis, Introduction, in Plato, *Five Great Dialogues*, 7.

30. Creation Studies Institute, "Quotes About Jesus Christ," www.creationstudies.org/Education/quotes-about-jesus.html.

31. Augustine, quoted in J. Gilchrist Lawson, comp., *Greatest Thoughts About Jesus Christ* (New York: Richard R. Smith, 1930, orig. pub. 1919), 59.

32. Jean-Jacques Rousseau, *Profession of Faith of a Savoyard Vicar* (New York: Peter Eckler, 1889), 103–4.

33. Editors of baroquemusic.org, *Johann Sebastian Bach: His Life and Work*, PDF download (n.p.: New Horizon e-Publishers, n.d.), 25, http://www.newhorizonebooks.com/DLB05Johann SebastianBach.pdf.

34. Napoleon Bonaparte, quoted in John B. C. Abbott, "Napoleon Bonaparte, December 10, 1815," in *Harper's New Monthly Magazine*, 10 (December 1854–May 1855): 177–79.

35. Vincent Van Gogh, *The Complete Letters of Vincent Van Gogh: Volume III* (Boston: New York Graphic Society, 1978), 499.

36. Lord Byron, quoted in Herbert W. Morris, *Testimony of the Ages or Confirmation of the Scriptures* (Philadelphia: J. C. McCurdy, 1880), 737.

37. H. G. Wells, "The Three Greatest Men in History," *Reader's Digest*, May 1935, 12–13.

38. Charles Dickens, *The Letters of Charles Dickens*, ed. Graham Storey, vol. 12, 1868–1870 (New York: Oxford University Press, 2002), 12:188.

39. Daniel Webster, quoted in J. Gilchrist Lawson, comp., *Greatest Thoughts About Jesus Christ* (New York: Richard R. Smith, 1930, orig. pub. 1919), 133.

40. *Select Speeches of Daniel Webster, 1817–1845* (Boston: D. C. Heath, 1893), 391.

41. George Bancroft, quoted in J. Gilchrist Lawson, comp., *Greatest Thoughts About Jesus Christ* (New York: Richard R. Smith, 1930, orig. pub. 1919), 121.

42. Dr. Irmhild Baerend translated from original text. David Friederich Strauss, "Vergängliches und Bleibendes im Christenhum," 1838; also quoted in Philip Schaff, *The Person of Christ: The Miracle of History, with a Reply to Strauss and Renan and a Collection of Testimonies of Unbelievers* (Boston: The American Tract Society), 341.

43. Schaff, *The Person of Christ*, 48–49.

44. Ernest Renan, *The Life of Jesus* (New York: Random House /Modern Library, 1955), 65, 393.

45. Sholem Asch, quoted in Ben Siegel, *The Controversial Sholem Asch: An Introduction to His Fiction* (Bowling Green, OH: Bowling Green University Popular Press, 1976), 148.

46. Sholem Asch, quoted in Frank S. Mead, ed. and comp., *The Encyclopedia of Religious Quotations* (Westwood, NJ: Fleming H. Revell Company, 1965), 49.

47. William Albright, *Archaeology and Religion of Israel* (Baltimore: Johns Hopkins Press, 1968, orig. pub. 1942), 176.

48. Nelson Glueck, *Rivers in the Desert: A History of the Negev* (New York: Grove Press, Inc., 1959), 31.

49. Kenneth Scott Latourette, *A History of Christianity*, vol. 1, *Beginnings to 1500*, rev. ed. (San Francisco: HarperSanFrancisco, 1975), 35, 44.

50. Mahatma Gandhi, *Gandhi on Non-Violence*, ed. Thomas Merton (New York: New Directions, 1965), 34.

51. Pinchas Lapide, *Jewish Monotheism and Christian Trinitarian Doctrine*, A Dialogue by Pinchas Lapide and Jürgen, trans. Leonard Swidler (Philadelphia: Fortress Press, 1981), 59.

52. Charles Malik, "These Things I Believe," http://www.orthodox .cn/catechesis/thesethingsibelieve_en.htm.

53. Malik, "Jesus Christ's Effect on Politics," Why-Jesus.com, http://www.why-jesus.com/politics.htm.

54. Kenneth L. Woodward, "2000 Years of Jesus," *Newsweek*, March 28, 1999, 55, reprinted in *The Daily Beast*, http://www.thedailybeast .com/newsweek/1999/03/28/2000-years-of-jesus.html.

55. *Charlton Heston Presents the Bible: Jesus of Nazareth*, DVD, Charlton Heston, actor, dir. Tony Westman (Burbank, CA: Warner Home Video, 2011), back cover.

56. Laura Alsop, "Decoding da Vinci: How a Lost Leonardo Was Found," CNN Living, November 7, 2011, http://www.cnn.com /2011/11/04/living/discovering-leonardo-salvator-mundi /index.html.

57. *Materializing Religion: Expression, Performance and Ritual*, eds. Elisabeth Arweck and William Keenan (Hampshire, England: Ashgate Publishing Limited, 2006), 166; Roy Greenhill, Sr., "Handel's *Messiah* Word Book, © 1998, http://tks.org/HANDEL /Messiah.htm.

58. Charlie, "Handel's Messiah: A Brief History," AnotherThink: One Christian's View of Post-Modern Life (blog), http://www .anotherthink.com/contents/movies_books_music/20051218 _handels_messiah_a_brief_history.html.

59. George Frideric Handel, "I Know That My Redeemer Liveth," http://www.tsrocks.com/h/handel_texts/aria_i_know_that _my_redeemer_liveth.html; to hear the music, look for one of the numerous performances on YouTube.

60. G. S. Viereck, "What Life Means to Einstein," *Saturday Evening Post*, October 26, 1929, 117. A transcript of this interview can be found online at http://www.einsteinandreligion.com /einsteinonjesus.html.

61. Pat Miller, "Death of a Genius," *Life*, May 2, 1955, 64.

62. Peter Larson, quoted in David C. McCasland, "God Intrudes," *Our Daily Bread*, December 12, 2006, http://odb.org/2006/12/12 /god-intrudes.

63. Unknown author, quoted in "Quotes about Jesus Christ," Creation Studies Institute, http://www.creationstudies.org /Education/quotes-about-jesus.html.

CHAPTER 3

1. Time, 3 December 1990, 45.

CHAPTER 5

1. Quoted in Michael Battle, *Practicing Reconciliation in a Violent World* (New York: Morehouse, 2005).

CHAPTER 6

1. Charlotte Elliott, "Just As I Am Without One Plea," https://hymnary .org/text/just_as_i_am_without_one_plea#Author.

ABOUT THE AUTHOR

B illy Graham, world-renowned preacher, evangelist, and author, delivered the Gospel message to more people face-to-face than anyone in history and ministered on every continent of the world in almost 200 countries and territories. His ministry extended far beyond stadiums and arenas, utilizing radio, television, film, print media, wireless communications, and thirty-three books, all that still carry the Good News of God's redemptive love for mankind. Engraved on a simple fieldstone in the Memorial Prayer Garden where he is buried at the Billy Graham Library in Charlotte, North Carolina, these words exemplify how the man and the minister wished to be remembered: "Preacher of the Gospel of the Lord Jesus Christ."

STEPS TO PEACE WITH GOD

1. GOD'S PURPOSE: PEACE AND LIFE

God loves you and wants you to experience peace and life—abundant and eternal.

THE BIBLE SAYS ...

"We have peace with God through our Lord Jesus Christ." *Romans 5:1, NKJV*

"For God so loved the world that He gave His only begotten Son, that whoever believes in Him should not perish but have everlasting life." *John 3:16, NKJV*

"I have come that they may have life, and that they may have it more abundantly." *John 10:10, NKJV*

Since God planned for us to have peace and the abundant life right now, why are most people not having this experience?

2. OUR PROBLEM: SEPARATION FROM GOD

God created us in His own image to have an abundant life. He did not make us as robots to automatically love and obey Him, but gave us a will and a freedom of choice.

We chose to disobey God and go our own willful way. We still make this choice today. This results in separation from God.

THE BIBLE SAYS ...

"For all have sinned and fall short of the glory of God." *Romans 3:23, NKJV*

"For the wages of sin is death, but the gift of God is eternal life in Christ Jesus our Lord." *Romans 6:23, NKJV*

Our choice results in separation from God.

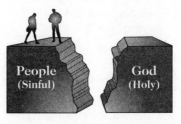

People (Sinful)

God (Holy)

Our Attempts

Through the ages, individuals have tried in many ways to bridge this gap ... without success ...

The Bible says ...

"There is a way that seems right to a man, but its end is the way of death."
Proverbs 14:12, NKJV

"But your iniquities have separated you from your God; and your sins have hidden His face from you, so that He will not hear."
Isaiah 59:2, NKJV

There is only one remedy for this problem of separation.

3. God's Remedy: The Cross

Jesus Christ is the only answer to this problem. He died on the cross and rose from the grave, paying the penalty for our sin and bridging the gap between God and people.

The Bible says ...

"For there is one God and one Mediator between God and men, the Man Christ Jesus."
1 Timothy 2:5, NKJV

"For Christ also suffered once for sins, the just for the unjust, that He might bring us to God."
1 Peter 3:18, NKJV

"But God shows his love for us in that while we were still sinners, Christ died for us." *Romans 5:8, ESV*

God has provided the only way ... we must make the choice ...

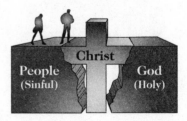

4. Our Response: Receive Christ

We must trust Jesus Christ and receive Him by personal invitation.

The Bible says ...

"Behold, I stand at the door and knock. If anyone hears My voice and opens the door, I will come in to him and dine with him, and he with Me." *Revelation 3:20, NKJV*

"But to all who did receive him, who believed in his name, he gave the right to become children of God." *John 1:12, ESV*

"If you confess with your mouth that Jesus is Lord and believe in your heart that God raised him from the dead, you will be saved." *Romans 10:9, ESV*

Are you here ... or here?

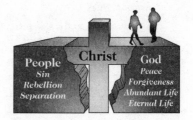

Is there any good reason why you cannot receive Jesus Christ right now?

How to Receive Christ:

1. Admit your need (say, "I am a sinner").
2. Be willing to turn from your sins (repent) and ask for God's forgiveness.
3. Believe that Jesus Christ died for you on the cross and rose from the grave.
4. Through prayer, invite Jesus Christ to come in and control your life through the Holy Spirit (receive Jesus as Lord and Savior).

What to Pray:

Dear God,
    I know that I am a sinner. I want to turn from my sins, and I ask for Your forgiveness. I believe that Jesus Christ is Your Son. I believe He died for my sins and that You raised Him to life. I want Him to come into my heart and to take control of my life. I want to trust Jesus as my Savior and follow Him as my Lord from this day forward.

                In Jesus' Name, amen.

_____   _____
Date   Signature

GOD'S ASSURANCE: HIS WORD

IF YOU PRAYED THIS PRAYER,

THE BIBLE SAYS ...

"For 'everyone who calls on the name of the Lord will be saved.'"
Romans 10:13, ESV

Did you sincerely ask Jesus Christ to come into your life? Where is He right now? What has He given you?

"For by grace you have been saved through faith. And this is not your own doing; it is the gift of God, not a result of works, so that no one may boast." *Ephesians 2:8–9, ESV*

THE BIBLE SAYS ...

"He who has the Son has life; he who does not have the Son of God does not have life. These things I have written to you who believe in the name of the Son of God, that you may know that you have eternal life, and that you may continue to believe in the name of the Son of God."
1 John 5:12–13, NKJV

Receiving Christ, we are born into God's family through the supernatural work of the Holy Spirit, who indwells every believer. This is called regeneration or the "new birth."

This is just the beginning of a wonderful new life in Christ. To deepen this relationship you should:

1. Read your Bible every day to know Christ better.
2. Talk to God in prayer every day.
3. Tell others about Christ.
4. Worship, fellowship, and serve with other Christians in a church where Christ is preached.
5. As Christ's representative in a needy world, demonstrate your new life by your love and concern for others.

God bless you as you do.

Franklin Graham

If you want further help in the decision you have made, write to:
Billy Graham Evangelistic Association
1 Billy Graham Parkway, Charlotte, NC 28201-0001

1-877-2GRAHAM (1-877-247-2426)
BillyGraham.org/commitment

A DYING WORLD NEEDS THE HOPE OF JESUS CHRIST.

There are more people alive today without the hope of Jesus than ever before. Together, let's reach them—in our communities and across the globe—with the Good News and tell them about *"the riches of the glory of this mystery, which is Christ in you, the hope of glory"* (Colossians 1:27, ESV). Since our founding in 1950, this has been our singular mission.

To find out how you can offer the hope of Christ to our lost and dying world, visit **BillyGraham.org** today.

BILLY GRAHAM
Evangelistic Association
Always Good News.

©2020 BGEA